Daughters of the King Stop Kissing Frogs

PAMELA HORNE

HIS GLORY
CREATIONS PUBLISHING LLC

www.hisglorycreationspublishing.com

ISBN: 978-1-950861-24-8

Scripture references are used with permission from Zondervan via Biblegateway.com

Printed in the United States of America
10 9 8 7 6 5 4 3 2 1

ACKNOWLEDGMENTS

First, I give Glory, Honor and Praise to my Lord and Savior Jesus Christ.

Thanks to my former Pastor and Aunt, the late Dr. Mae V. Horne for her prayers, teaching, impartation and speaking over my life.

Thanks to my parents Frank and Bessie Horne for raising me to believe in my abilities.

Thanks To the late Al Wiggins, my favorite college professor who instilled in me confidence in my gift to write and went out on a limb to make sure I graduated.

Thanks to my cousin Joyce Horne Waller and all my family and friends who pushed me to publish my writing over the years. Thanks to my cousin Jaqueline Barnes for purchasing the first copy of my first book. Special thanks to Tina Thompson who has been my biggest cheerleader.

Thanks to my Sissy, Daphne who continues to push, believe in and support and my brother Martin for setting up my office and reminding me that I am supposed to write.

Thanks and Love to all my brothers, Frank, Thomas, Martin and Will; my sisters Melanie and Leanne and my big sister, the late Felecia Harris for being an inspiration.

Thanks to the Women of Triumph and Elder Anna Lyons for their support. Thanks, Minister Diane Pace for lighting the fuse and encouraging me to start writing.

Thanks to Pastor Marian Freeman- Weaver and the Gateway to Heaven UHC family and all those who supported me.

Last but not least, thank you, Minister Felicia Lucas and His Glory Creations Publishing Company for helping me realize my dream.

DEDICATION

This book is dedicated to all the Daughters of the King who finally know who they are in Christ and are waiting on God's promise... It may not come when you want, but it will be right on time!

Table of Contents

Preface

Daughter of the King Arise! You are royalty, not a novelty. Stop allowing yourself to be treated like a toy. Stop allowing yourself to be toyed with. Represent your Father, be about His business. Get in the Word! Prepare yourself for your King. Get in the Word! Study to show thyself approved. Stop allowing frogs to draw your attention away. Stay focused. You are royalty. You are not a novelty that a man plays with until tired. Your Father has groomed you for a king. Stop kissing frogs and hoping they will turn into Princes. Everything you have been through has been in preparation for your King. If you never marry, God is your Father-the King of Kings. Don't be sidetracked by a good-looking, smooth-talking frog. You can kiss him and kiss him and kiss him, and he'll still say "ribbit." Only an encounter with God can change that. You can't do it, so stop trying. Frogs represent unclean spirits. You can't fix them. If you marry them, you will be torn between pleasing them and pleasing your father. God didn't want his children yoked together with unbelievers because they would turn away from serving Him and be drawn away to idols. You're royalty, a daughter of the King. Wait on your king, the Priest of your home, the one God has prepared for you. Stop trying to piece together a man using frog parts.

Introduction

Galatians 3:26-29 So in Christ Jesus, you are all children of God through faith, for all of you who were baptized into Christ have clothed yourselves with Christ. There is neither Jew nor Gentile, neither slave nor free, nor is there male and female, for you are all one in Christ Jesus. If you belong to Christ, then you are Abraham's seed and heirs according to the promise.

Romans 8:14 For those who are led by the Spirit of God are the children of God.

II Corinthians 6:18 And will be a Father unto you, and ye shall be my sons and daughters, saith the Lord Almighty.

Galatians 4:6 Because you are his sons, God sent the Spirit of his Son into our hearts, the Spirit who calls out, "Abba, Father."

Jesus undoubtedly shocked and even disturbed some of his followers and listeners when he addressed God not as just "Father," but "Abba" – Dear Daddy. It's a term reserved for that deep, lifelong connection between father and child. There's nothing formal about it, either, but it is sincere and full of love and understanding. As adopted children, we are welcome to approach

God the same way. We may call him "Father" to show respect, but the Holy Spirit allows us to have that intimate understanding and connection to be able to call him "Dear Daddy," too.

Other religions see God as one to be feared, respected and honored. He isn't approachable as a father and child relationship. There's distance and barriers that they think should always separate us from the Almighty. But Jesus showed us that true sons and daughters, even adopted ones, do have that privilege. Our God is not just the king, but he's our daddy too. He wants to hear about our day. He wants to comfort us and be our security when we're scared. He wants to talk to us while we go through difficult trials and tribulations and give us wise advice. No matter our age, he sees us as his children and welcomes us to sit next to him and talk to Him like we talk to our father.

A novelty is a small and inexpensive toy or ornament, a knickknack, trinket, toy, trifle, ornament, etc. Novelty is the quality or state of being new, different, and interesting: something that is new or unusual: something novel: something unusual and entertaining that is popular for a short period of time. Novelties wear off. Royalty is the status of an elite class. Royalty has royal status, dignity, or power; sovereignty.

Princess is a regal rank and the feminine equivalent of prince (from Latin *princeps*, meaning principal citizen). Most often, the term has been used for the consort (wife) of a prince or for the daughters of a king or sovereign prince. Princesses, or daughters of other suitably high-ranking nobles, were used as political pawns to gain power and forge alliances. From childhood many girls were promised to kings, and many marriages occurred before the princess reached her teenage years. The young women were uprooted from their homes and sent to other kingdoms to be married, and they would often never return home again. Esther was taken from her home to eventually become Queen of Persia.

Marriages were the ultimate political alliances, and they were seen to be permanent (divorce was not acceptable in the Middle Ages), and children created from the union become heirs to two kingdoms. The primary purpose of a princess or young queen was to produce an heir, more specifically, a male heir. Daughters were valuable for forging other alliances.

God wants what's best for his daughters. He is not looking to marry you off to someone who doesn't believe in Him. He's not looking to marry you off to a man that is going to abuse you. He's not looking to marry you off to a man that is going to disrespect you. God values his daughters. As daughters of the King, we have to value ourselves.

Abraham, knowing God's wishes, forbade Isaac to marry a Canaanite. Isaac, in turn, did the same with his son Jacob. Intermarriage could have led Jacob into embracing the evil ways of the land. That would have led his immediate descendants into embracing idolatry and the other immoral ways of the Canaanites. Such compromises would have led to God's pouring His wrath upon them within a few generations.

The King's daughters lived a life of privilege. They were well protected and groomed for royal men. As daughters of the King, we have to be virtuous women. We can't expect a Prince or a king if we have no restraint or virtue about ourselves. We must know who we are, and we must command respect from men.

Princesses would spend a lot of time on religious activities. They would attend chapel several times a day and spend time studying the bible - Princesses would often be taught to read and write (a rarity in those days). Depending on their age, they would also have lessons. The feminine arts were the main lessons— music, singing, dancing, sewing, embroidering and maybe drawing or painting. Languages were also a big part of lessons. Princesses were "bought and sold" internationally on the marriage market, so languages were important for when they moved abroad to marry a foreign prince. Latin and French were mainly taught, but Italian, Spanish, German etc., may be taught as well. Princesses would often help the sick and the poor.

When we accept the Lord Jesus Christ as our Savior, we become daughters of the King and obtain the privilege and responsibility of representing Him in every area of our lives. However, we must claim that position before we can walk in it. We are all His daughters! Don't allow the enemy to continue to hold you back from all God has for you. Accept your identity and begin to walk in it! Princesses possess a positive influence. Every little girl dreams of and wants to be a princess. As a daughter of the King, you have the power to influence and mold other young women of the kingdom. Have a positive attitude that will determine the people you will meet, the jobs you'll get, the friends you'll keep, and the blessings you'll receive. Your attitude will determine how high you go in life and what you'll achieve.

Princesses possess confidence. They know who they are and whose they are. They know where they are going in life and that no man can stop what God has promised. Princesses know their worth. They know they are worth more than gold. They can't be purchased or commercialized. They appreciate other sisters, lift up others and are concerned about souls.

Jesus was the best thing that happened to me. It was years before I would understand that Jesus loved me and that I was of a royal priesthood, a chosen generation. I was a Daughter of the King of Kings and the Lord of Lords, and I would no longer continue to "Kiss Frogs." You see, I kissed many "Frogs" in my life, trying to turn them into a prince. Born one of eight children and raised in a religious family in North Carolina, I made it through many years of anguish and pain to get to Him! Just to get to Jesus! When I look back over my life, I realize that the things people go through is for their making.

My mother was a great homemaker and cook. She took care of us while my father served in the US Navy. I remember his ship, the USS Kitty Hawk and living in Massachusetts. Moving back to North Carolina at an early age changed my life forever. My father was stationed away from us and not a constant authority figure in the home. This made a great difference for us as we navigated our way through life. My mother would discipline us, and 6 months later, when Daddy came home on shore leave, she would run down the list of what we had done, and we would get it again. I would think, hey, mama already spanked us six months ago for this. No matter, Daddy was home, and we had to answer again.

Submerging ourselves in my father's family church also changed my life. My mother started taking us to church with her on a regular basis. My father was stationed in Virginia, and we lived in North Carolina. He came home for 30 days here and there but never long enough. We started singing in the choir. I also started Ushering. I never thought I would end up preaching the Gospel of Jesus Christ, let alone being ordained as a Pastor, but those early years were preparing me for the future.

My brother was born and was very sick. He spent the first few years of his life in a Navy hospital on Fort Bragg. We didn't see him much until he was about two. At two, he looked four. That's how big he was from the steroid shots. He had seizures as a child, and the Doctors said he wouldn't live past the age of eight.

He was a cutie pie, and my mother relied on the church's prayers and the healing virtue of God to save him. He was her miracle baby. We all got close to God around that time and exercised our faith in that situation. By the age of two or three, I remember he was able to come home for weekend visits. I remember him lying in the crib and having seizures. We eventually brought him home to live with us a few years later. My sister and I had to help Mama take care of him and give him his daily shots. I had to help Mama hold him while my older sister gave him the shot. He was terrified every time he saw the needle. When my mother started playing the keyboard for the choir, she would sit my brother beside her, and he would play everything she played. He played by ear. He didn't start school until he was about seven.

I was content to be a good girl, attend church regularly, and sing soprano in the choir. That was as deep as my relationship went, and it was that lack of knowledge that led me away from everything I had been taught to hold as right in life. I wasn't prepared for the real world and the weeping and mourning that would accompany it. I had been sheltered, and now it was time to make my own decisions, and I didn't always choose the right thing to do. By the time I reached High school, I was tired of being different from everyone else. My friends even sheltered me from things they didn't think I could handle. They knew I wasn't going to come to any parties, so they didn't invite me. Surely, I wasn't going to rebel against my parents and sneak out.

My first date in high school was with my boyfriend and his father. Yeah, his father came with him to pick me up, and we went to church. Believe it or not, that was a big deal to me. I sang in the gospel choir in High school, and eventually, I was allowed more freedom. He was allowed to take me out, and I could ride with him to and from practice. I thought he was the type of guy that was perfect for me. He even talked about being a preacher. Like any teenaged boy, his hormones were out of control, and he made it clear what he wanted. We even debated the Bible about it. Girls, once you have any sexual contact with a guy at that age, he will think he owns you. By the end of the year, he had to go. The final straw was when he wouldn't take no for an answer. We were on a group outing at a cookout in the park, walking through a wooded path, when it happened. I resisted him, and we struggled. I was screaming no, but he wasn't hearing me. I remember seeing another guy walking through the woods, but he didn't help me.

After that day, I knew it was over as soon as he got me home and I told him I didn't want to be with him anymore. He had planned our lives out and wanted me to go to a local college so we could get married right after high school. I had other plans, and as long as I was with him, I wasn't in control of anything. He ended up moving away to live with his grandmother, but he still called me to try and patch things up. I stopped taking his calls, and sometimes he would come by around the holidays to see me. Years later, we would finally talk about this incident and put it behind us, but I was in my thirties before I could forgive him and move on.

By the time I started college, I was doing what was right in my own eyes and not consulting God. Being on my own, I placed myself in many compromising situations. These events shaped my future and destiny. Remember, when you go through that, All things work together for the good of them that love the Lord-**Romans 8:28**. I couldn't see it then, but now I understand. Some things I went through so that others wouldn't have to. My biggest regret and source of anguish was finding myself a freshman in college, in love with "Lee" and pregnant by someone else. You see, before I met him, I had been in two compromising situations. The first one, I narrowly escaped being raped, and the next, I gave in to get it over with. He was the father, and all I could think about was my life was over. I didn't want to be with him. We talked about it, and he begged me to have the baby. He had worked out a solution where we both could finish school and see the baby on the weekends. My life would never be the same. I could never tell my parents this, I would lose Lee, and in my mind, there was no other solution. I wanted my life back, so I decided to have an abortion.

That day, at the table, I talked to God and I begged him to forgive me. That's when I decided I couldn't do it. I wanted my baby. For the first time, it was real to me. I began to get off the table when the Doctor held me down, and in a voice from hell, he said, "You better be still. It's too late. You be still and let me finish or you'll never have another child again." **Death and Life are in the power of the tongue-Proverbs 18:21**. That Doctor spoke death over me that day. After it was over, I never got pregnant again that I know of. "Lee" found out, and I eventually lost him anyway. This incident fueled my desire to die and fed my deep depression over the years. Whenever a man would do me wrong, I figured I deserved it. I didn't care about myself after all this. Over the years, the weight packed on, and I looked for men that could make me whole again. I wanted to be fixed. I would have occasional nightmares about the baby and wake up screaming or crying. In my dreams, I always imagined a little boy.

I drank a lot at parties and social occasions because it was the only thing that helped me interact with people. I pretty much took every drug that was placed before me except one. Prince's song had a line in it about crack. You remember, "Crack killed Applejack. "When it hit campus, I had almost finished school, and I had started to get more serious about my grades. I wasn't hanging out as much or doing drugs. They didn't seem to get me high anyway. I didn't like cocaine, speed or rush, so I stuck with marijuana and alcohol. That was the college norm, believe it or not. Let's get back to crack. Crack had some of the girls doing anything to have it. These were all rumors, but when I was over at a friend's, I saw those girls in the back room with a bunch of guys, and every time the door opened, a billow of smoke would come out. I knew it wasn't weed smoke, and I wondered what it was. My friend said, "You don't want to go back there. That's not for you." He wouldn't say what they were smoking, but I knew. I went to that door, but I didn't walk through it.

God shielded me from that drug that day. My life had to take a different turn. It was tempting. I longed for a hit of anything that could make me forget. Lee was there that day. We would get together whenever he came back for homecoming or occasional visits. He had graduated my sophomore year and was working for a company in California. I was still infatuated, and every time I saw big Lee, it was as if no one else existed. My friend knew this, and he would make sure he got us together when he came. We could never get past the past, and a lot of things had happened in between that drove us farther apart. My bad decisions mostly. We had hurt each other a lot. He had been my best friend, and I loved him. His death in 2013 left a void in my life that only God could fill.

This book is written to all the young women like me who have so much promise but allowed circumstances to divert their destiny in this world. The following chapters recount the years of my life that I wasted Kissing Frogs. Never allow anyone to hold any power over your life. No circumstance is too great that God cannot overcome it. Your story may be different, but everyone has their own cross to bear. Whatever your story is, God wants you to know that you can overcome it through him. And they overcame him by the blood of the Lamb and the Word of their testimony- *Rev 12:11*. If we are faithful believers, we overcome Satan by being free from his power. Speak the Word over your circumstances and serve the

Lord by sharing your testimony with others to strengthen them. When you share your testimony, the enemy can't use it to keep you bound. Most of the time, we do not want anyone to know what happened or things that we did. These skeletons cripple us in life because we are consumed with shame, but God wants to turn it around and use it for our good.

For I know the thoughts I think toward you saith the Lord, thoughts of peace, and not of evil, to give you an expected end- Jeremiah 29:11. God already had our destiny planned out, but he left it up to us to choose. We are the ones who knew the way but decided to take a different road. When we make the wrong decisions, the results are catastrophic. The smallest mistake can cause us years of regret. God can still take those messed up years and turn them around for our good. Remember, we walked down those roads in life, blaming God when we didn't seek him first. God wants us to have hope for our future. It's the enemy's job to convince us of the opposite, so we will remain in the dark. Daughters of The King, Stop Kissing Frogs!

CHAPTER ONE

The Charming But Deceptive Frog

*The Bible warns, **"Charm is deceptive" (Pro. 31:30), and "an enemy multiplies kisses" (Pro. 27:6). Gen 3:4 "You will not certainly die." The serpent said to the woman.***

Many women have said the gifts and attention their husbands showered on them while dating stopped not long after they got married. "What happened?" they wondered. Who we marry affects us, our parents, our siblings, our friends and our extended family for the rest of our lives. It's wise to consider where the character of the person will lead us down the road. How does he act towards people? Observe how he interacts with the waiter, his co-workers, and even his parents? A man of noble character may be rare but worth the wait. Who is the person beneath the charm?

Best friends don't come and go in your lifetime; they remain there, always near and prepared to step in when God's season comes for them to play roles in your life. My best friend Asia and I grew up together like sisters. I adopted her parents as my Godparents. Looking back, I didn't give them a choice. I just said, "you guys are my new Godparents," since I never knew mine. She sang in a group with her cousins, and we would fellowship with each other's churches. We were good church girls, but we soon became preoccupied with teenage issues and began to stretch out and secretly rebel against our straight-laced image. I wasn't as adventurous, fearing the flames of eternal hellfire if I really sinned, so I just puffed on cigarettes, not even knowing how to inhale.

The years that preceded those days had already been filled with childhood hurts that I was determined to overcome. Hurts that went back as early as 3 or 4, by what I could remember. I armed myself early and began to defend myself against the enemy as I saw him to be. Those were struggles that opened the doors to different spirits that I didn't even know were there. I always tried to remain in control of things. When I couldn't verbalize what I was going through, I acted out. I would play with razors, scratching, never cutting my wrists, but feeling a desire to do so. I was convinced that death would be the answer to escape my depression, but I was afraid of the consequences of suicide. I wanted to go on to be with Jesus. My frustrations led to rage. I was quick to pick up a butcher knife in defense of myself against any threat I perceived. My younger sister used to refuse to wash dishes and help clean up the house. It was my responsibility to get it done, so it all felt unfair. One day, she refused to wash dishes, and I snapped. As she sat on top of the washing machine taunting me, I grabbed her by the throat and began to choke her. My grip on her throat tightened, and I snatched her off the washing machine and took her to the floor with the intent to kill her that day. I don't know who pulled me off of her, but I remember feeling angry and tired of being in that house. It was only three-bedrooms, there was never any privacy, and my brothers and sisters seemed to always get their way, while I was overlooked and held responsible if things were not done.

When I started Jr. High, I got into cheerleading to get away from the house. That was one thing I could do since I couldn't play basketball like my other girlfriends. My first kiss was in the school cafeteria, and that was a big deal since I barely talked on the phone. Years later, he ended up saved and praying for me. All my old girlfriends ended up getting together years later at one of the girl's housewarming parties, and "Carla" was telling everybody about the team and the positions they played. She was our forward, and she played point guard and Pam, well, she was our cheerleader bless her heart. It was true. I wanted to play. I could shoot all day but couldn't run and dribble, no coordination.

Outside of games and practice, my friend would always joke that I could never go anywhere because I was always washing dishes. Think about it, eight kids and two adults. Every meal was a big production, and it felt like just about every pot, pan, and dish in the house needed to be washed. Most kids think they had it harder than their siblings; it's the nature of sibling rivalry. Those days of youthful innocence would soon be shattered by real-life struggles, which intensified as I got older.

I never felt anyone understood me, especially as a child. I have always felt that I loved people who couldn't return love or didn't know how to meet my standards of love. I gave all and ended up much too often with nothing in return. I've always been better alone to some extent since I was very quiet, extremely shy and not willing to risk rejection.

Asia was outspoken and just knew she was always right. She was a good friend, and we could talk about everything. She tried to change the way I dressed and wore my hair, but I only took bits of advice from her. I wasn't allowed much freedom in those days. Nevertheless, we were sisters, and I remember tossing and turning when I went off to college, and she told me about her new "boyfriend." As she began to talk about him, I began to have nightmares and pray for my friend. I was in a backslidden state myself, but I still loved the Lord and longed for his presence. He showed me things about this guy that I can't explain. All I know is- I went home on break, and we were at her parent's home when he showed up. I came out to the living room to meet this man, and all I saw was blackness. To this day, I don't recall anything about his face. "He was faceless and dark. I pulled her into her bedroom and burst out crying, pleading with her to get rid of him. He was the epitome of evil, and I knew his plans were to sift her as wheat! Praise God! She had started having doubts about him, and my reaction confirmed those doubts. It scared both of us what we found out later about this "PIMP." He was charming and deceptive, his motives were evil, and he even played the role in front of her God-fearing parents to put her at ease, but the warning signs were there.

Growing up, my parents were strict, and my father, who was retired from the Navy and taking his place in the home, was brutally "Frank." That happens to be his name. He was like James on Good Times, except he cursed like the sailor he was. I guess I took after him as I got older. I communicated with cursing and just being blunt. I still tell it like it is, that's just me. One thing is for sure! I never wanted to try my father because I believed he'd do just what he said. Like my grandfather always threatened, "Girl, I bet I'd put my foot on your neck until it snaps." Sure would make you grab your throat.

The best advice my father gave was never allow a man to take care of me. If I did, I would feel trapped. "Always take care of yourself, Sug. There ain't many men left like your father who will let you sit home and not work. Your mother worked when she wanted to help out, but I always took care of the family, and she raised the kids. I'm glad you are going to college; you can take care of yourself." My father and I would have heart to heart talks, and he would just be honest, sometimes too honest. I dyed my hair red in college, and he said, "You look like a floozy." That certainly dashed the fly image I had of myself. He was a hard man at times, not the same daddy who baked cookies with me and my girlfriends in Boston.

As children, he used to have us working in the garden every day planting something or picking beans, but I always knew he loved us. He was also the self-appointed neighborhood Dad. When he would come to school to pick my brother or me up from after school events, he wouldn't leave until he was sure the other kids had rides. He would wait around, and if no one showed up, Daddy would say, "Tell that boy to get in the car." I would relay the message with a "Hey, my Daddy said come on and get in the car, we're taking you home." We always had plenty of room in the Station wagon or Cadillac. He and mama always seemed to argue, and we always thought they were on the verge of divorce, but he'd say I can't afford to leave; I have to feed all you Cluckers! He had a point. There were eight of us after all.

My Daddy loved to fish of course, and he loved to take the kids with him, especially the boys. He was a father figure to my cousins, the favorite uncle, and took my brothers and cousins on fishing trips to the coast a lot. I just wanted to hang with Daddy, even though he wasn't big on watching us around water. I didn't care because Daddy would allow us to explore and play and make a mess and just be kids.

I remember in Boston, we went fishing with one of his Navy friends. Daddy was fishing a little ways off, but his friend was close by keeping an eye on me as I walked along the beach, playing on the rocks and scooping water into a can. I slipped and fell into the water and suddenly felt seaweed tangled around my legs. Something kept pulling me down as I struggled back and forth to the surface to yell, "Daddy, Daddy." I didn't know how to swim. I could see his friend with his hand extended, but I wanted my Daddy. I almost drowned that day while Daddy was still trying to reel in a fish. Fortunately, I came to my senses and took the man's hand. "Calm down, Sug, you're alright. Sit here and dry off. Don't tell your Mama or she won't ever let you go anywhere with Daddy again." I knew he didn't want Mama to know because he would be in serious trouble. When we got home, my mother took one look at my curly hair and knew I had been in the water, and of course, when she asked, "Pam, what happened to you," I quickly confessed, trying to reassure her that I was ok. All I could hear her say was, "Frank!" and I scattered. I would no longer get to go with

Daddy fishing because Mama was petrified that I'd end up drowned or something. She didn't trust my father to watch over me. If my older sister went, I could go, but that wasn't likely. She was a teenager and wasn't at all interested in fishing. She didn't want her little sister tagging along with her and her friends, so I had to make friends of my own. That was hard for an introvert like me. I was quiet and painfully shy. My friends just happened. There weren't too many black families in the neighborhood and not too many real friendly white families. I did have one white friend next door who was allowed to play with me. Eventually, I became friends with "Lila and Annie." They were a little older than me. They were the younger sisters of my older sister's best friend, "Dena." They used to come over, and Daddy would bake cookies with us. When we moved back to North Carolina, they moved to Louisiana, and I missed them a lot.

My brother and I were thicker than thieves. We should have been twins, but we were born a little over a year apart. When we got older, he teased and tortured me about my weight because he needed someone who would take his abuse. He no longer wanted to hang with his sister, he had friends. Trouble was, I was light-skinned with long hair and thick. I wasn't fat at the time, but I was on the heavier side compared to my friends. I was curvy and didn't even know it. Compared to them, I thought I needed to go on a diet. I had no idea how shapely I really was.

People you love have the ability to pick up on your insecurities and use them against you. My brother had me convinced I was fat. He was supposed to be my friend when no one else would. He would say, "I'm sorry," but his words would already have caused damage beyond repair. One thing about him, he didn't let anyone mess with me at school. That's how it was with older brothers, they felt like they had the right to pick on you, but of course, no one else could.

He and my older brother used to have to walk me to and from school every day. They sure didn't like it though. I remember Jr. made me run behind him, threatening to leave me. I was in first grade and scared. Running as fast as I could with my books in my hand, I slipped and fell into mud. I was covered from my shirt to my socks. He had to take me home crying and mud-covered. I was mad because it was a new outfit, and it was all ruined.

In Jr. High, my brother was the all-around athlete, and I was a cheerleader. Most of the girls who didn't like me put up with me because they were crazy about my brother. I still had a lot of enemies. Those were the days when I prayed a lot for people. I had anger built up in me stemming from things that I had kept inside and allowed to fester, but I learned to turn them over to God. Long before, What Would Jesus Do bracelets, I learned to consider him in all my ways. I guess that's how I dealt with people who had hurt me and learned to discern the ones who I needed to stay away from. Yes, I could discern a person's spirit at an early age. I didn't know it was discerning, but I just knew which people to steer clear of. Some people I couldn't avoid, so I always remained vigilant whenever they were around. Kissy lived down the street, and she was older than I was. She used to hang with the boys, but she wouldn't let me follow her. In her own way, she made sure she looked out for me.

My self-esteem was so low that I didn't know how to have a healthy relationship. I didn't trust men, and I had to put myself out there when I met the one with whom I thought I could have everything I ever wanted. We worked in the same field, corrections. It was good because he worked at the Federal prison, and he wasn't from North Carolina. He was patient and played the role of the perfect guy. He even told me that he wanted an honest relationship and confessed that he had always cheated on past girlfriends. He basically told me straight up **I AM A CHEATER,** and I still chose to trust him completely. Caution- When a man tells you who he is, believe him the first time! He was sweet, but I learned that I had trusted someone who wasn't worthy of being trusted. He had women in Virginia, back home, in New York, and under my nose; etc.; he was just a cheater. That breakup got ugly because he left me for someone else. The only thing that made me feel better was knowing that he was cheating on her worse than he had ever done me. She deserved it, I thought. After all, she knew about me. Why do we put ourselves through drama? Yes, the agony of these relationships was something I put myself through, and I was angry with myself for years. The Charming, Deceptive Frog always hurts the most. He's the Great Pretender that works overtime to get you to trust him and lulls you into a false sense of security, leading you to believe "Everything's Lovely" in your relationship then pulls the rug out from under you with, "lately I just don't think we want the same things" or "it's not you it's me." No, it's not them, it's you- as I learned through this process of Kissing Frogs, I was the one that picked him!

CHAPTER TWO

Discerning of Spirits:
The Angry Abusive Frog

"Do not make friends with a hot-tempered person, do not associate with one easily angered, or you may learn their ways and get yourself ensnared" (Pro. 22:24-25). "An angry person stirs up conflict, and a hot-tempered person commits many sins" (Pro. 29:22). "A man without self-control is like a city broken into and left without walls" (Pro. 25:28)

Living with an angry person is like walking through a minefield. The meal he loved yesterday irks him today. Rage isn't the only sign of anger. Cutting comments and sarcastic jokes are enough to leave you feeling bad. Before long, you doubt yourself. His anger will rob your joy as surely as the stomach flu steals your appetite. Scripture warns, life happens. You need a spouse who can handle disappointment, not one that will crush your children's spirits or foster angry teens.

From as early as I remember, I would have this recurring nightmare where I was floating above my aunt's backyard in Virginia, looking down at myself as a toddler. I was walking around the yard and picking up something on the ground. Suddenly, I couldn't breathe, and as my spirit was leaving my body, my mother would run up to me and frantically start pulling at my nose. I would wake up in a sweat over this dream for years. One day, I shared this dream with my mother, who looked astonished at the detail I gave her. She said, "Pam, there is no way you remember that. You were only about 18 months old, barely even walking." "So, this really happened," I asked? She would go on to explain that I was in my aunt's backyard, and I was walking around picking up acorns and stuffing them up my nose until I couldn't breathe. When she saw me struggling to breathe, she ran up to me, and she was panicking, trying to pull those acorns out of my nose.

My mother describes me as a very different child. I was quiet and content from the start. She told me that when I came home from the hospital that she and my father thought something was wrong with me, but they couldn't figure it out. After three days, they realized that they had not heard me cry. Panic set in as they started to imagine all sorts of things. They finally concluded that I must be deaf and mute. My parents decided to pinch me and see what happened. I finally cried, and they were relieved. Even as a small child, my mother said she could give me a toy, sit me in a corner, and I would play all day. Very introverted from the start, I liked having my alone time. I had my own room until my sister came along and eventually moved in. I didn't adjust to this very well. I wanted to be alone.

I can also remember a white woman with long hair past her waist that took us in her house when our car broke down. She allowed my mother to heat up the baby bottle while my father and her husband worked on the car. My mother claimed that happened in Washington State, and I was only six months old at the time. I don't know how I can remember these incidents at such an early age. Now, it seems like I struggle to remember things that happened a couple of months ago.

Around the second grade, I remember a boy who never talked. He would just sit there and stare through you whenever you spoke to him. I always tried to be nice to others, but this boy was disturbed! My teacher used to take the class to the library and read to us at one of the tables. I had on a dress that day, and that boy sat next to me. All of a sudden, I felt him thrust his hand up my skirt. I started hitting him in the head, trying to make him turn me loose. He just sat there and stared straight ahead. He had one hand on me and the other on the girl sitting on the opposite side. The teacher told me to stop hitting him and sit back down. I refused to sit beside him, and I got up and moved. I thought about running home but feared I'd get in trouble if I did. I never told anyone, but I suspected the teacher knew. She just didn't care. She was old and clearly focused on retiring. I couldn't tell my mother, and my father wasn't home. I stayed away from that boy whenever I went to school. He was emotionally disturbed, to say the least, and I didn't trust him. Clearly, he had some things going on at home, some dark, abusive things that had manifested in anger and perversion. I never heard from him again after that year, and I always wondered who he became. He had the makings of a serial killer for sure.

I got out of a lot of things by playing dumb. My first time being allowed to ride my bike through the neighborhood was with one of my friends. She decided to bike through a path that took us a couple of streets over to another neighborhood. We were chased by a couple of boys in the path. She got away, and I got caught. They didn't hurt me because they knew my brothers, but they sure scared me. It was more like the spirit in one of those boys that scared me. I knew what he was about. His eyes told me what was lurking in his mind. They let me go, and I went on my way and caught up with my friend. Of course, I wouldn't tell this story. I'd never get out the house again. That same boy would start hanging out at the house with my brothers and leering at me every chance he got. His sister was one of my friends at school, and she was wild. I wasn't much for pretending that I liked you if I didn't. I couldn't always explain why I didn't care for certain ones, but I just knew I didn't trust them. Later, I would learn to separate the spirit in that person from the person while still remaining vigilant.

There was one incident that I remember when I was about eleven. I saw what I would later identify as a "Butch" spirit for the first time. She was an older relative of the family that I was visiting. She immediately came in and tried to bully us and tell us what to do. Mind you, she was too old to be hanging around us younger girls in the first place, but no one noticed. I was aware of the spirit lurking behind her eyes, and I was vigilant and on-guard. All I remember for sure was I didn't trust her, and I had seen that spirit before. Years later, I would identify it as **Perversion**. The dictionary defines perversion as the alteration of something from its original course, meaning, or state to a distortion or corruption of what was first intended. She tried to touch me, and I started swinging and ran out the room. This enraged her, and she made the other kids turn on me, male and female. Years later, I would run into this person at a gathering. She was "married" to a woman that I worked with at the time. I kept my distance, thinking, "she don't even remember who I am." I didn't say anything, but I thought, "small world," and with that said, I put it behind me.

I remember many instances and conversations with loved ones, warning them of this spirit after recognizing it in operation. Young ladies, please don't play with this spirit. Keep your distance because it will try to attach itself to you so it can enter. I have seen this spirit and studied how it operates and transforms young girls from sweet little girls to brutish, boy-like mutants or submissives while parents shrugged off the behavior as she's just going through a Tomboy phase. It is a spirit, and it operates in control and instilling fear, clearly nothing to play with. Make it clear. Don't be persuaded by this spirit. It will kill you. Most of these controlling relationships end violently.

Someone I knew was trying to get herself together and draw closer to God after years of drug abuse. She had a woman living with her, and she was trying to get away from her. It's not easy to get out of these relationships. Tragically, she was stabbed to death. This was devastating to the family because her life was finally taking a turn for the better. The woman who killed her had killed twice before, been to prison twice, and released to kill again. Sadly, she didn't get much time for her murder, and she will one day likely be free to do it again. Angry, abusive Frogs surface in all types of relationships.

One of the best ways to discern a spirit is to consult the Word of God. What does the Word say? What is the person saying or doing? Does it line up with the Word or is it in direct contradiction to the Word. People with spirits of perversion are evident to me, even the men and women who proclaim to love the Lord. I could see that spirit on a Gospel Artist every time I saw him gyrating to gospel music on TV. "It is something about him that I just can't stand to look at him," I would say to others. I knew it was perversion, but I didn't know it was addiction to pornography until he revealed it on TV one day. "That's what it was," I thought. I'm still not a big fan, but I don't get the same reaction when I see him.

A well-known Bishop was another one that bothered me. His muscle shirts and muscle-flexing didn't fly with me. I would watch him preach, but I couldn't get past those muscles. Why is he parading his physique in the pulpit, I wondered? It bothered me, and whenever I saw him, it was weird, but I would always think of a certain football player who was rumored to be Bisexual. They favored, and more importantly, they had the same spirit. Eventually, it would be revealed through public accusations that it was a spirit of perversion. I believe that God can turn any situation around and deliver you from anything. One admitted his struggle, and he was delivered. The other never did admit to his faults publicly, but only God knows. That was between him and God ultimately. No man can judge you, and no one has a heaven or hell to put you in but God. Sometimes people with callings on their lives will struggle with things that they try to hide from others. Instead of admitting and confronting their demons, they bury them and move forward. When this spirit decides to resurface, and they have not been delivered, they are not able to resist the temptation. It is sad to see the man of God and his ministry fall. Many churches don't provide for deliverance in their ministries. Sadly, there are many who are leading the people and preaching a good word, but they are in need of deliverance. They have large followings, and the love of money persuades them to compromise with sin in order to keep the big money and tithes flowing. They are guilty of the blood of those who they are leading. If they keep quiet about certain things, they enjoy the financial freedom that these people bring and the big churches they are able to build. Unfortunately, these churches are helping the communities on the surface but not providing for the spiritual needs of the people. For what shall it profit a man, if he shall gain the whole world and lose his own soul- *Mark 8:36*.

Telling a person the truth, that's love. I learned not to beat anyone over the head with the Word but simply to love and let the love of God shine through me. When I'm asked about what the Bible says, I tell them. I give them the Word of God. These people out here preaching inclusionary doctrines that lead people to believe that they are alright with God and that they are not sinning are causing millions to die in their sins and lose their souls. Love them enough to tell them the truth and pray for them while they are lost. Sin is sin, and no sin will enter in! The Holy Spirit is so grieved by these false teachers and Demonic Shepherds who care about money more than souls. They are caught up in hearing their own voice instead of God's. God said for us to turn from our wicked ways.

I heard a well-known preacher poses the question, "Will Homosexuals go to Heaven?" When the question was posed to another preacher, I didn't hear either of them condemn the practice itself. One of the preachers put it like this, technically it is fornication, and the Bible is clear that we should not fornicate, so that makes it a sin. I'm sorry, but the people need to hear the truth. Homosexuality is a sin. Well, if you are not saying that it is a sin, then you are leading them to believe that if they marry, then it's ok. It's time to take a stand for the Word of God. All these big Pastors skating around the issue in order to keep the money rolling in are going to roll around with that money in Hell. Those who don't want to stop doing what they are doing and twist the bible to justify their lifestyles will have to answer to God. It is not man's decision to say that it is not a sin. It is God's. He has already spoken, and no man can change that. My thoughts are not your thoughts, neither are my ways your ways- *Isa. 55:8*. It is a spirit and if you are struggling with it, God can deliver you. God did not create you to be this way. Behold, I was shapen in iniquity and in sin did my mother conceive me- *Psa. 51:5.* We were all born in sin and shapen in iniquity. If I didn't love you, I would not tell you the truth. It is not an option for any of my loved ones to be lost. Give it to God and allow Him to deliver you. Get into the Word and stay there. You may fall, but we all do that. Acknowledge God in all your ways and He will direct you.

Asia had married and settled down not far away, but she had become obsessed with Jesus and church. I was single and still partying, not yet, I'd say. I was running from Jesus, and I didn't want to be convicted of my wrong. Asia couldn't possibly understand what it was like for me because she was married and settled in life. I thought I would get married first and then settle down. I wasn't ready yet. I needed to get myself together. That's what I told myself. Every time I went around her, she was preaching Jesus, and I just wanted to spend time with my old friend. Soon, we went our separate ways but kept in touch over the years.

I only went to church on special occasions, and that was enough for me. It seemed like everyone was getting "religion," but me at that time. I would pray in times of trouble, but I don't think I ever picked up my Bible the church had given me for graduation from High School. I can't be like those people who had never done anything wrong in their life. I was the biggest sinner in the world compared to them. This is what I thought. Not knowing that most of those saved, sanctified and Holy Ghost filled saints actually had checkered pasts much like mine, some had gone through much worse. I would never have thought that God could use me, or even wanted to. Boy, was I wrong about all of it? All have sinned and come short of the glory of God! I always had my own relationship with God. It just wasn't as intimate as it would become one day. I always believed in God, but I wanted to come clean before I came back to Him. This was something I didn't realize at the time, that I would never be able to do. He was going to have to do the cleaning, not me. He's still cleaning me. It's a process that will continue until I die. If only I had realized that years ago, I would have come back to Jesus sooner. It's never too late to give your life to Him. He's the best thing that ever happened in my life.

People have a way of turning their noses up at you and making you think that you are a hopeless case. Don't believe the hype. That's just that self-righteous spirit operating in them. The Apostle Paul said that he was the chief of sinners. Imagine the one person who persecuted the Christians the most, had them tortured, killed and thrown in prison, suddenly has a change of heart. He became the biggest Christian of them all. He wasn't received at first; people were still leery of him, and they wouldn't forgive him of his past. God still used the Apostle Paul to write the majority of the New Testament. It is not up to people, it's up to God. God allowed me to see that one of the sisters in the church had a jealous spirit over me. I could literally see the spirit behind her eyes. I did my best to show her love and allowed her space to get delivered from the way she felt. She was constantly testing me. Sometimes, she just made me mad, and I didn't pass all those tests. During one of our services, she came to me crying and asked me to forgive her for being so jealous of me. That was God that day. Although she continued to struggle with it, she confessed that fault and we were able to get along much better. I learned a lesson from her about confessing your faults and humbling yourself.

God used dreams to show me what spirits were operating in me. For all have sinned and come short of the glory of God- *Romans 3:23.* Don't think for one minute that you are perfect. We all talk too much, and we can all be consumed with ourselves. Whenever God would convict me for things that I had done to hurt someone else, I would go to them and repent. Sometimes you need to take a look at yourself, discern your own spirit. People use the gift of discerning as an excuse not to deal with others. They say that they discerned your spirit, and the Holy Ghost told them to watch out for you. Suspicion of people is not discernment. Most of the time, the ones you push away are the ones who God has sent to help you. Don't become so self-righteous that you listen to yourself more than God.

Sometimes God will warn you about people, but you need to know when it is God and when it is flesh. Flesh will have you judging people and forgetting where he brought you from. People are in need of deliverance, not judgment. When they come into the church, it is our job to help them through their deliverance. What if someone hadn't taken time with you? So many times, we write people off as if there is no help for them. ***God is our refuge and strength, a very present help in trouble- Psalms 46:1.*** God never leaves our side, and we can call on him when we need him. His grace is sufficient for any circumstance of life. There's nothing too big for God. I read a book about a woman who was high up in witchcraft. She was sent to destroy a Christian woman. Although this woman knew who she was and what her assignment was, she shared Jesus with her anyway. Eventually, the witch saw that God was God and Satan was a liar. She ended up converting to Christianity and becoming a witness for Christ. "He Came To Set The Captives Free," by Rebecca Brown, M.D. is a very powerful book. It is a testimony of these two women's experience. She was a witch, a regional bride of Satan, and she had knowledge that Satan didn't want the people to hear.

I had unknowingly opened doors throughout my life for the enemy to come in. I never even realized what I had done. Many people buy into the belief that certain sins are going to send them to hell or because they have done certain things, they are already doomed to go to hell, or they have sold their soul. That's what Satan wants you to believe. Satan can't buy your soul. Jesus already paid the price. The only way for Satan to get your soul is if you give it to him by refusing to live for Christ. If you are not saved, Satan already has your soul; he just works that much harder to keep it by keeping you from the truth. Certainly, the woman in the book bowed to Satan and made him her master, but when Jesus came into her life, he became her new Master, her Savior and Lord. There's nothing too hard for God. She went through this so that she could be a testimony to draw others out of witchcraft and win them over to Christ. God loves us no matter what we have done. It's never too late to get it right.

Spiritually, my eyes, ears and nose began to become sensitive to different spirits. I could see the spirit in the eyes of the person, hear the spirit speaking through the person or smell the foul odor that the spirit gave off. I also began to be able to sense the presence of evil. When you are in the presence of evil, you must maintain a level of spirituality where you don't allow the enemy to pull you out of character. I have seen a loved one possessed by evil, and because I was not in position, that spirit ran rampant and wreaked much havoc that day. You see, I allowed the enemy to get me angry, and when the time came, I was not in a spiritual position to pray against that spirit. It was a spirit of rage, and murder was its intent. It wasn't the person I knew. It was demonic and strong.

The person's eyes were red and evil, like something out of a movie. The only time I would see something like this was when my Pastor would be casting the Devil out of people. I've heard Jailhouse stories about people who snap and kill or commit other heinous crimes. When they come in, they seem possessed by evil. Some family members have come in and said, "I don't know who that is, but it's not my brother." They don't understand what happened to the person they knew and loved. These people are possessed, and sometimes Christian staff have to pray and cast out those spirits. Unfortunately, the Devil made me do it is not a defense. I've seen people possessed, and they fight with five or more staff members and send some to the hospital. These are not huge people most of the time, but they have supernatural strength.

As I started following the ministry under my Apostle's leadership, God started revealing people that were manifesting demons. The first one I remember is a female who was in line for prayer. As she got closer to the man of God, she began to tremble, her face contorted, and she started making a shrieking noise. Others in line didn't seem to notice, but I said to myself, "That Ain't God." The Holy Ghost drew my attention in, and I started praying. There have been several occasions where they would start manifesting, and I would know that he was getting ready to cast them out. I have seen people slither on the floor like snakes, perch on all fours, hiss and move like a cat, speak in deep, demonic voices and scream out no, not you! The demons sometimes laugh and say they are not coming out, etc. Let God arise, let his enemies be scattered: let them also that hate him flee before him- *Psalm 68:1.* Being part of a Deliverance Ministry is different from attending a regular church. I've always been in Deliverance ministries, but this one is more intense. These churches that have large numbers are fun to be part of, entertaining in some aspects and nothing is wrong with that. Bottom line, if they are not operating in Deliverance, the people are still bound. God showed me a dream of a church with stadium-like seating. It was pretty large. He showed me that the people were coming in wearing orange jumpsuits, handcuffs and shackles on their feet. They were bound by sin, and some of them were sitting with their lovers, two women, two men, etc. The name of the church I was looking for was Genesis, but I ended up at this place. Some of the details, including the name of this church and date when it was formed, coincided with the description of a church body that decided to ordain gays in their organization. God was showing me the condition of the church and what direction it was headed in. He had me searching for Genesis or the beginning, trying to show me that the people needed to get back to their first love, how they reverenced God in the beginning. The people were being entertained and led to believe they were alright. They were not alright, they were spiritually bound by sin, and being led astray. God was showing me co-workers and what they were involved in. They were like prisoners, who were flooding into the sanctuary with prison clothes and restraints on. They were not worshipping God because they were not in true fellowship with God. God is a spirit, and they that worship him must worship him in spirit and truth- *John 4:24*. Confession of sin is clearly important to worshipping God. If your doctrine sets aside the truth of God, it has no foundation in God. ***A liar is of the synagogue of Satan- Rev. 3:9.***

Angry and abusive relationships take many forms. The angry and abusive person can tear you down with their mouth, beat you down with their fists or mentally abuse you. When you kiss an Angry and Abusive Frog, you believe that your love will change them. Your love will be their saving grace. Women internalize abuse and start believing they deserve bad treatment.

After trying to date my boyfriend from a distance, we decided I would relocate to live with him until we could get settled. I overlooked many signs that he had changed because I wanted to hold on to the image I had of this perfect man. I had no clue who he was. Even when he held a gun to my head and threatened to kill me "cheating...." because he was high and out of control and paranoid, I rationalized this and blamed it on the substance. I never cheated on him. I knew the gun didn't fire, but it was one of those moments where I felt like it was meant to go off this time. As I looked at the gun pointed at my head, I caught the eye of an auburn -colored horse. Yes, it was a horse, and it represented the hatred he felt for me at that time. I thought I was hallucinating, but one of the neighbors was riding up on that horse. Looking into the eye of that horse, my life flashed before me, and I resigned myself to the possibility of dying. The person before me was driven by a passion and desire to destroy me. It was pure evil I was faced with. As I looked into the eye of that horse, I somehow knew that I had the ability to face this challenge. I remained calm, and I talked to him and took the gun from him.

As I unloaded the gun, my friend and her boyfriend, who were visiting at the time, begged me to leave with them, and they would put me on a bus home. I refused to go, reassuring them that I would be ok. The truth was I was afraid to go and afraid to stay but convinced I could fix this; I could fix him. Please, ladies, hear me when I say this, you can't fix him, you can't even fix yourself. Only God can do that for you.

Nevertheless, I stayed with him. We were engaged to be married, and he kept putting off the date. One day I just realized that he didn't want to get married. I threw the ring at him, and he took that as his way out. I kept in contact over the years, but I only saw him once after that. We never saw each other again. After this relationship ended, I went through the next eleven years being in one bad relationship after the next.

CHAPTER THREE

Soul Ties- The Lazy, Unproductive Frog

*The Scripture says, **"One who is slack in his work is brother to one who destroys" (Proverbs 18:9).** How many people have lost their families, careers, and souls through laziness? **The parable of the talents called the idle servant "wicked" and "lazy" (Matt. 25:26).** These strong words are spoken with good reason. Sloths are parasites to society and their families. Paul wrote, **"The one who is unwilling to work shall not eat" (2 Thes. 3:10). Laziness often hides behind unreasonable fears and excuses (Pro. 26:13).***** *Steer clear of a lazy man.*

Apathy damages our character, hinders our growth, and robs God and those with whom we live and work. Those who ignore their responsibilities damage their team's morale and effectiveness. A spouse who is too lethargic to invest in his marriage or share the load of rearing children drains the whole family.

My senior year in college, I began dating a guy that treated me so good that I loved him from the start. He was my friend, and he seemed to get me, I thought. I trusted him completely and never thought he would tell me anything wrong. My roommate and I shared an apartment off-campus.

One of our neighbors was majoring in the same area I was. She and her roommate were very friendly, and they would come by from time to time. One night, they came by and brought a "board "game for us to play. When I discovered it was an Ouija board, I quickly objected. I had never seen one, but I heard it was evil. The girls assured me that it was just a game, but it was not until my boyfriend convinced me that he used to play it with his aunt and that it was harmless that I decided to play with them. The board had the alphabet across the top, the words yes and no, some numbers, and occultic symbols from what I could remember. We were instructed to place our index finger lightly touching the game piece, and when the neighbor started asking questions, a freaky thing occurred: the piece started moving and spelling out words by the alphabet. Yes and No answers were answered by pointing to yes or no on the board.

The person asking the questions asked, "Who are you?" The board spelled out DAVID and said he was nine years old and died in 1908. Eventually, I learned that it was a spirit we were communicating with that was attached to the board. This spirit was very mischievous, and it would play tricks on us. One night it sent us into a frenzy when we thought my roommate's boyfriend had been in an accident. It told us he was by the new coliseum. We jumped in the car and took off in search of his car or any signs of an accident. We didn't find one. When we returned to the apartment to ask it more details, it spelled out HAH HAH HAH HAH

HAH HAH! This scared me, and I didn't want anything else to do with this game.

My roommate and others continued playing with the board on two separate occasions. The "game" was intriguing, especially when it spelled out one of my professor's names and said he loved my neighbor. "Bailey" loves "Leah," "Bailey" loves "Leah," it said. She said, I don't know why he's so crazy about me, but it's true. This man was my absolute worst nightmare in school. He had influence over the radio station, school paper and taught two classes that I had to pass to graduate. I had passed one class, and this was my last year in college, my last semester, and I was taking the second class. It was Television production II. We weren't required to go to class, just show up for tests. We also had to go to labs. All I had to do was shoot and edit my own commercial or 30-second spot. If I did 4, I got an A; 3, and I got a B; 2 and I got a C and just one for a D. I went for the D. Anything to avoid being in the presence of this man I feared so much.

My work-study job was spent as the Department receptionist. All the Department Professors would come in to get their mail out of their boxes, and he would come in nearly every day and threaten to flunk me. "I'll see you in summer school Ms. Horne'" he would bark. This placed me under so much mental stress that I had to go to the infirmary. You see, if I didn't pass this class, I didn't graduate in May. I would have to take the class over the summer or wait a whole year before it was offered again. There was no other professor who taught this course, so I had to go through him. The thought of him having a soft spot for anyone was sickening. My favorite professor had an office on the opposite side of this man, and I would run into him a lot.

Towards the end of the semester, I began shooting my commercial. It was about smoking, and I had to get some of my friends to help out. I was having trouble getting the footage because the battery packs kept dying. Finally, I got the footage I needed, and all I had left to do was edit the project. One glitch, and he said he would flunk it. One week before graduation, and he flunked my project. When he said, "I'll see you in summer school, Ms. Horne," I blanked! I don't know what all I said, cursed or threatened, but I unleashed all the anger, frustration, rage and disgust I felt for him. I told him he was a miserable son of a....., and he was an intimidating bully who I couldn't stand to be around. I must have threatened him. I don't remember, but one of my sorority sisters was there, and she told me he was pretty shaken up after I left, and he went out to check his car. The truth is, if I had known how to make a car bomb or even known what type of car he drove, I would have messed it up that day, probably shredded the tire with my teeth if I had to. I had no fear of going to jail, not in that county. The inmates sunbathed on the lawn of the courthouse and even answered the phone when you called down there. That's another story.

I had murderous thoughts about this man, I must confess. I rushed out of the lab in tears, screaming and crying, and sat down in the stairwell, totally distraught. While I was sitting there, several of the other professors who had heard the commotion came by and asked me if I was alright. Incoherent and inconsolable, I just wailed. One of the professors handed me some tissue and asked, "What did that miserable Son of a ***** do to you?" They were more concerned with me than him. They didn't like him either. This had ruined my life as I saw it. My boyfriend came and picked me up. He assured me that everything would be fine. We could live together while I took the class over the summer. He was really not focused on school, and he had no real drive. He wasn't really focused on graduating. He was content to have a job and apartment off-campus, and he really wasn't going to classes. He was lazy and unproductive, and I was trying to push him to finish what he had started, but his mother blamed me for being a distraction. He didn't see my dilemma because he wasn't in a rush to graduate, and he was kind of glad that I wasn't going anywhere.

I called home and told my mother I wouldn't be graduating and relived the horrible episode. She must have got the church to pray because the next day, my favorite professor came by to see me and told me not to worry. There was a convention over the weekend before graduation for all the students and staff who were members of the radio fraternity. I wasn't part of this or anything else he was part of, so I wasn't going. He assured me he would take care of things. My neighbor, "Leah," also came by and said, "Don't worry, Pam, I'll talk to him this weekend."

They both came back that Sunday night with news! My professor slipped a note under my door, which said I was going to get another chance to edit my project, be there in the lab by 1:00 the following day. That Monday, I went in and I was calm and cordial to him and I finished. There was a slight glitch, and he pointed it out and asked," now, what do you think your grade should be?" I started crying and said, you're going to flunk it. He said, "You passed Ms. Horne." When he said that, a wave of emotion and excitement came over me, and I grabbed him, hugged him, and said thank you. He said, "See, I'm not as bad as you thought I was." I graduated three days later.

When I returned home and started job hunting, I couldn't get a good job because I didn't have a car or a driver's license, just a permit. This really crippled me because the job I had waiting for me at a local radio station was in sales, and I couldn't take it.

My relationship didn't work out, and eventually, I moved on. I finally let my guard down and started being friends with a co-worker. He knew how fragile I was, and he played that caring role from the beginning. You see, when I met him, it had been a year since my breakup, and I hadn't dated anyone because I was still reeling from the pain of making wedding plans and being hurt by the one I thought I loved. Men always hurt me.

That relationship with my co-worker ended up taking me to the brink of insanity and back. When I look back on those days, I remember hearing voices that drove me to act totally out of character. He kept me so mixed up with his mind games that I wanted to hurt him, even kill him at times. I know what it's like to snap. He listened to everything I wanted, down to the type of house I wanted, and then he gave it to another woman.

One bad relationship after another consistently being led on and ending with him married to someone else. These relationships produced soul ties. Even my best friend hurt me. He was the one I truly loved, but he would never commit, so I moved on. We stayed in contact with each other over the years and started seeing each other when we could. No strings attached, except my heartstrings. He never told me he was getting married. I met him down at the beach during bike week, not knowing that this was his bachelor's party weekend. When I called a couple of weeks later, his mother said, "He got married, didn't he tell you, Pam?" Crushed cannot describe this blow. I never quite recovered from this. This was not the first time something like this had happened, nor was it the last.

I met a guy through a friend. We were having a reunion and also celebrating my sorority sister's wedding. She was having a reception for family and friends. While hanging out and playing cards at my other sister's boyfriend's house, this guy started talking to me. I was busy drinking shots of Tequila and beating everybody in spades. He kept trying to engage me in conversation, and he told me that he could read palms since he was a little boy. "Can I read your palm, "he asked? My reply was no. I remember him picking up the Bible and telling me some stuff about Adam and Eve. He seemed to know scripture pretty well, but what he was saying somehow sounded twisted to someone who had worked her way through shot number 14. I remember telling him to put the Bible down because I didn't play with the Lord. He finally grabbed my hand and started reading my palm. I don't know why I gave him my number, but I did. He lived two hours away, and I wasn't really into him.

It turns out, he was a Worshipful Master of a lodge. He was a Mason and a schoolteacher. What kept me at bay with him was his preoccupation with things like palm reading and keeping exotic pets like, for instance, his albino python, which he tried to tell me had died, but reportedly it was still alive and allowed to roam freely through his house. He also had an iguana. When he told me of the three dogs he had that were part Rottweiler and part Pit Bull, needless to say, I never went to his house. I did meet him halfway a couple of times to go out, and he came to Durham once to see me.

The first time he met me halfway, he said he had left his wallet at home. I thought to myself, he's crazy if he thinks I'm paying. He made a few calls, and not too long after, a man came by and brought him enough cash to pay for the date that evening. This was one of his Masonic connections. I believe this whole scene was orchestrated to impress me with how much power he appeared to have. I was curious to know if what I had heard about the Masons was true, so I asked him. I looked at him, and I asked, "Are the Masons involved in witchcraft?" He looked at me and said, "Yes, it is witchcraft... It depends on how high you go in the organization. The higher you go, the more you get into certain rituals that are based on witchcraft."

I knew he grew up with a grandfather who was a preacher and also a Mason. I knew he was very familiar with the Bible, and I could see he was fascinated with exotic pets and occultic things such as palm reading. What I didn't know and failed to ask is why he remained part of an organization that practiced witchcraft? We talked over the phone a lot, and he expressed his desire to marry me within a couple of months, but I was not interested. This man was settled in life, he had his own home and career, etc., but something was off. I couldn't get past his pets and refused to meet them, ever!

Some years later, God would lead me to study these organizations. I know what the Lord revealed to me and why I wasn't drawn to him. I also know why he was drawn to me. The Masons follow a Luciferian doctrine written into all Scottish rite rituals that is based on the belief that there are two co-equal Gods. Lucifer, they believe, is the god of good and light, while the Christian god, Adonnay, is the god of evil and darkness. They believe that one cannot exist without the other, and the struggle between good and evil is what balances out the Universe. They pray to the Grand Architect of the Universe, but they are praying to Lucifer and don't even believe it. This isn't revealed until the thirty-third degree of Masonry. If I handed you a human skull and said to you, drink from this skull, you would probably think it is witchcraft.

They take oaths that curse their children and generations to come. That's what he meant when he told me that it was witchcraft involved at higher levels. Why were the men involved in this type of activity so quick to want to commit to me? Apparently, family members on both sides had been involved in these organizations, so it was a generational curse that was following or pursuing me through these men. Much of this would not be revealed to me until much later, as the Holy Spirit directed me to seek out the truth through scripture and studying. I pray that those of you who read this and are involved in any organization would study and research it for yourself. Acknowledge God first and ask the Holy Spirit to lead you into truth. You can't depend on what someone else says. You must have the revelation for yourself. I had to come to the conclusion for myself and only God could have shown me. If you love the Lord, and you want to be pleasing in his sight, choose this day to serve him only. He is God, and he is God, alone.

Years earlier, there was a guy who was older and a divorced father of one who tried to marry me after two months. He was a 9th-degree black belt in Karate and 9th-degree black sash in Kung Fu. He used to tell me that he was a Ninja, and he could walk through walls. Now I thought this was foolishness, and because I didn't understand the spiritual realm and how witchcraft worked, I didn't pay him much attention.

I was in college, and he would come up to visit me on weekends. Sometimes I would call home during the week to find that he was hanging out with my family visiting. My mother thought it was a little weird, and so did I. After two months of dating him, I decided I was feeling a little tied down, and he was pressuring me to marry him and transferring to a college closer to home where he lived. I wasn't interested in giving up my whole life, and I didn't know him well enough to marry him.

The prospect of becoming someone's nineteen-year-old wife and stepmother to his child did not appeal to me. I wasn't ready for that. I had barely began living, and I was hardly through with partying and hanging with friends. I knew that I was on the rebound from Lee anyway, and he wasn't over his ex-wife. "This is absolutely ludicrous, "I thought. We argued the night before he was supposed to go home. I told him it was not working out, and it was over. That night I slept in my roommate's top bunk while he slept on the bottom. I remember tossing and turning, finally waking up at 2 a.m. I screamed in horror at this ghastly looking figure hovering over my bed looking at me. It was gray and dressed in one of those hooded robes like you would see a monk wearing. It reached out at me with a long bony, withered-looking finger and tried to touch me.

When I screamed, it dissipated. My boyfriend never woke up. When I shook and kicked him and tried to wake him up, he didn't move. That's when I realized that he had something to do with that thing that came after me. I would learn later that witches and warlocks practiced what is known as astral projection, where they could go into a trance and send their spirit into other areas. This happened to also be a practice of Ninjas. It was him. He was the ugly little monster in the room that night. That's why I couldn't wake him. I know it sounds crazy, hard to believe, but I couldn't make this stuff up. It's the truth. I've often wondered since then what his intentions were that night. What was he trying to do to me? A couple of months later, he came by my mom's and showed my sister a picture of his new wife. He had known her for six weeks. It's not that people can't meet and fall in love within six weeks, but I couldn't see it.

There were certain beliefs that had been planted in me throughout life that kept me from making the worst mistake of my life. I thought it was a cruel twist of fate that I ended up single and childless, but it was all orchestrated by God. "Lil Man" was divorced, ex-military and the one that I could never tame. He was a challenge to me. Over a six-year period, I was back and forth with him. He was one that I fell back on when other relationships didn't quite work out. I remember being on the rebound from one guy and "Lil Man" came by. We talked, and he expressed that he did love me and wanted to be with me, but he had something to tell me. What he told me hurt deeply. He had another girl pregnant. She was due in a couple of weeks, but they were not together. What? He had always been adamant that he did not want children, and I knew he had no problems, so there must be something wrong with me. I forgave him because we weren't together when this happened, but it still cut like a knife. I caught him over and over again, cheating, so I stopped expecting more from him.

In those days, I was consumed with finding out what was going on and my mind was always racing. I was suspicious about everything and having trouble sleeping because my mind was racing. Two years earlier, I had been in his apartment and saw a familiar name on his caller ID. I dismissed it because I figured since they had worked together, that's how they met. I never thought about it until two years later when I woke up at 2:00 am. I can't explain it, but there was an overwhelming drive for me to find out the truth. You see, he was a truck driver, and I knew he was in town, but where? Her name came to mind, and it was like some voice in my head was screaming that name at me. I looked in the phone book, and there was her number. I called her up, she answered, and I said, "Can I speak to "Lil Man?" He answered the phone, and we immediately started arguing. He couldn't understand how I knew where to find him and was angry that I called him out.

We could never get it together, and we separated again. The last straw with him was finding out through a friend that he had fathered another child. She was an old high school girlfriend that he had a fling with. There was another girl and pregnancy in the past. This time he was determined to keep this child a secret from me. He planned to let some other man raise his daughter. I begged him not to do that, but he didn't want another child support obligation. "He's not her father. You don't know what will happen to her if you're not there to protect her," I cried. I pleaded with him. We cried. He begged me to forgive him and I did. However, we went our separate ways after this. I didn't know what he decided to do. A year later, I rededicated my life to Christ. Now I know that the time will come one day for me to find true love, and I am persuaded that nothing shall separate me from the love of God.

Soul ties can only be broken by God. For most of my life, my struggle was with soul ties. None of these men loved me. I've never experienced true love. The counterfeit love that I received over the years was nothing compared to the love I experienced through Christ. He will never leave you nor forsake you. Lil man and I could never get it together, and my self-esteem was so low with him that I allowed him to literally stomp on me. I always seemed to inflict punishment on myself in those relationships.

Kissing a bunch of Lazy, Unproductive Frogs. It was almost like a drug. You hear of people cutting themselves to feel pain. They say it is the only way they feel alive. It was always something wrong with me, not them. Nothing that any man could do to me ever felt undeserved. Not until Jesus came into my life did I see that I deserved to be loved. Not until I released my baby to God would I finally begin to heal. My hope is in the Lord. Not until I released my baby was I able to come out of a deep depression. I had highs and lows over the years, but I never knew what it felt like to really be loved. I settled for the counterfeit feeling and resigned myself to the belief that what I had was as good as it gets. Why should I hold on to the belief that there was more? I couldn't let myself off that easily. Not until Jesus came into my heart did I begin to truly love myself.

CHAPTER FOUR

Favor Ain't Fair:
The Religious Frog

"For such are false apostles, deceitful workers, transforming themselves into apostles of Christ. And no wonder! For Satan himself transforms himself into an angel of light." (2 Cor. 11:13-14) "The religious spirit is out to imitate the work of the Holy Spirit and is concerned with outside appearances of being holy and righteous. The warning in 2 Corinthians 6:14, 'Do not be yoked together with unbelievers. For... what fellowship can light have with darkness?' deals with a person's essence, not his or her profession of faith.

There is a difference between having a religion and enjoying a relationship with Christ." ***Perhaps the man you're interested in started attending church with you. Maybe he is active in ministry. But is he hungry to know God? Does he love Jesus and people? Religious activity and a heart for God are not the same. "The Pharisees, who were the pastors and Bible teachers of Jesus's day, were hyper-religious. They also reeked of self-righteousness and lacked the mark of true faith—love for God and people.

The years 2000 -2002 were some of the lowest points in my life. It all started on Christmas Eve. I was working, and I had just hung up the phone from talking to my Mother. About fifteen minutes later, my cousin called and said, "I'm on my way to pick you up, your parents' house is on fire." No, the house can't be on fire," I said to myself. I had just talked to my mother, and everything was fine. When we arrived in the neighborhood, the street was blocked off by the fire trucks. We parked on the next street over and walked towards the house. Immediately, I saw my mother standing in front of the neighbor's house wrapped in a blanket. Immediately I wrapped my arms around her and cried with her. That house wasn't much, but there were many memories there. It was special to the whole family and to the neighborhood kids also. My cousin, who had picked me up, had lived there with us. My mother and father helped raise a lot of people and even watched some of the neighborhood kids. We always had a yard full of kids at our house, and the kids were close. Many of the neighbors came by to make sure my mother was ok. After the fire, they came by to board up the house for her. They loved the old house too.

The fire started in my parents' room, sparked by a floor heater. By the time she got off the phone with me and walked into her room, the fire was blazing. They tried to fight the flames, but they had to get out quickly. My nephew was only two years old. When Daddy told him to get out of the house, he moved. The neighbor's son picked him up and held him safely in the front yard. Other neighbors called 911 to report the fire. My parents soon gave up and left the house to wait for the fire trucks. Thank God, no one was hurt. My sister, her husband and children came as soon as they could get there. Her son was about four years old, and he kept asking about his presents that were in the house under the Christmas tree. Everything was basically destroyed in front of the house. What wasn't destroyed by fire was destroyed by water. It was a disaster, totally devastating to sift through the ashes and debris left behind.

My cousin and I lived across the street from each other. I had a three-bedroom house, and my sister, her son and my cousin were living there with me. I wanted to help them out until they could get themselves settled. My parents moved into my cousin's house, into her small spare bedroom. My brother camped out on the couch at my house. My father had had a stroke a few months earlier, fell out on the pier and hit his head. He was having spells where he was falling down. We found out that he needed to have surgery on his neck because there was a nerve pressing down that threatened to paralyze him if he didn't get a section of bone removed. My cousin decided to move out so that I could move my parents to my house. I gave them my bedroom; it had a king-sized bed and plenty of room for Daddy to move around on his walker.

My new room was the smallest bedroom. There was only enough room for a bed and a dresser. My parents were not given enough insurance money to rebuild the house, only enough to fix the damage. They were swindled out of their insurance money by some contractors who promised them a four-bedroom house with a full basement, etc., etc. "Mama, I don't trust them. This sounds too good to be true," I said. They were builders in Virginia, and they said they wanted to use mama's house as a model home for their new housing development. That's why they were giving her this great deal.

My cousin started working with them, and everything seemed to be legitimate. They began holding seminars at our family church and trying to get people approved for financing. There was always this gnawing feeling that something was still not quite right. My mother gave them $9,000 upfront to clear the lot. A family friend offered to tear down the house for the wood and hardwood floors. He also got the garage and shed that was not damaged in the fire. Once they tore the house down, there were piles of trash that needed to be cleared. The builders brought a small ditch witch and started clearing some of the debris. They never returned to finish clearing the lot and never started on the house. I found out later that Mama had decided at the last minute to get the basement. They told her she needed to pay for the basement walls upfront because it wasn't in the contract. My parents had given them $10,000 more.

After a little investigation, we found out that they had ordered basement walls, but they weren't for my parents. They took my parents money and finished another project in Virginia. Yes, they were legitimate builders in Virginia, but they swindled my parents. It turns out, they weren't licensed to build in N.C. They were legitimate builders in Virginia. They attempted to get my parents to allow them to continue and offered to build the house under another General Contractor in Durham. The problem was that the house price went up, they weren't getting a basement, and they now had to pay additional money to the General Contractor. My parents demanded their money back, but of course, they didn't get a dime. They ended up taking the case to court, and they won a judgment against them for three times that amount, but we could never find them to collect. Meanwhile, my parents used the rest of their insurance money to pay attorney's fees and additional money to hire someone to clear the lot. This ordeal took almost two years to play out, and my parents ended up with no money, a mortgage to pay on a house which was gone, and no other choice but to build a modular on the lot.

Those two years were full of ups and downs, unimaginable stress, and frustration that led me to drink and smoke more than usual. When I came home from work, my house was always filled with visitors. I couldn't relax in my own home, and I needed an outlet. When I ran into "him" at the Drugstore, he seemed so promising. We quickly became close, and he started spending most of his time at my house. On weekends, we started going to Virginia to play the lottery and hang out. He was my only outlet. I started gambling more frequently. It was the rush that I got that addicted me. I ran up about $15,000 in credit card debts trying to get away and escape the reality of my life. Everyone was jobless, and my parents could only help me with as much as they could. It would have been enough if there weren't so many people living there, running up bills and breaking things in my house. He was the only one I felt I could talk to and cry to. He was a car salesman and grew up in Durham. I believed he had potential, but again, he needed a little fixing. I overlooked his quirky behavior, even his preoccupation with candles and incense burning. He came to me one day and said his ex-girlfriend had worked witchcraft on him and caused him to lose good jobs, and he had gone downhill ever since. He was in a frenzy and begged me to drive him to South Carolina to see this man that could help him. His ex-girlfriend had him arrested soon after we met, and he insisted that she was mad because he had moved on. I believed him at the time, having no reason not to. He was afraid of going to jail for this, and he seemed like he was at the end of his rope. I was afraid he was cracking up. After he begged and pressured me to take him, I gave in. I drove him there about three or four times, and I always stayed in my car while he went in. I don't know what they did in there, and I only saw the man once. His office was in a work shed behind his house. One day, he came out of his house and walked towards the shed. As I watched him, I noticed that there was something strange about the way he moved. When I looked at his feet, they didn't appear to be touching the ground. Of course, my mind was tripping, or so I thought. I didn't like the look of the three dogs walking around behind the fence either. They were not natural looking. They reminded me of the dogs in the movie Incredible Hulk. They were huge and demonic-looking. I had to use the bathroom that day, and I went into the waiting room area to use it. I saw all these pictures of Jesus on the wall, like the cheap ones people usually hang on the walls in their house. I wondered about that. It seemed like a contradiction to his business. He was a root doctor, after all. I immediately returned to my car and waited for my boyfriend. Eventually, he got tired of giving this man his money, so he stopped going to see him. I was relieved that he seemed to be getting better. Then, he started focusing on herbal stores. My Doctor had sent me to an herbalist to get some medication to clear up a rash. She told me that it was the cause of my bad scarring after surgery. She was set to do another surgery to revise the scars but wanted to make sure the skin rash cleared up first. I thought something was strange about the place, but it was set up like a regular nutritional store. At the counter, I noticed there were business cards for a Spiritual counselor, and I think it was advertised on the door that Spiritual counseling was available. The woman seemed nice enough and said she had gotten interested in herbal remedies after working as a nurse and seeing what the additives in food was doing to our bodies. I remember that the owner of the herbal store my boyfriend used to like to go to in Greensboro said the same thing. After my boyfriend went to the store with me, he pointed out that the spiritual counselor was a witch. He showed me a magazine where the woman advertised. I wondered why he had the magazine and started to wonder if the shop owner was a witch also. Did my Doctor send me there because she was afraid I was going to sue her for malpractice? The pressure of his growing fascination with herbal remedies, candles, etc., came to a head when I found out that he was taking Wicca classes. He was also studying to be a warlock. He would light a candle and get in the bathtub of the hotel room and start praying in tongues. I could fix this, I thought, he's just a little mixed up. He comes from a good family. He has a God-fearing mother. I can fix this. Why do we convince ourselves of such foolishness? He had placed pennies in all my windows in my house. He would burn incense and go from room to room, cleansing the bad spirits or something. How can Satan cast out Satan? All the signs were there, but I couldn't see them at the time. My sister noticed the pennies, and she had asked a friend what it meant. She said he was trying to keep me in the house or under his control. He ended our relationship for a 23-year-old lookalike of his ex-girlfriend. He wanted her back the whole time. I went on with my life and rededicated my life to Christ.

When he found out I was saved, he started following me around and showing up where I was. My girlfriend and I were in her store when he just walked in. He had looked for me in every store after he saw my car. Once, he found me sitting in a restaurant with my friend's son. She was getting her nails done, and I had taken him to get some ice cream. He came in and sat down. I was still weak, and I fell for his friendship ploy. I came to my senses when he asked me to go to dinner with him. He seemed very distant that night and wouldn't tell me what was wrong. I dropped him off at his car, and he called about a couple of days later. We had a bad connection, and I didn't hear from him for two weeks. I had prayed that God would save him or break that tie. I prayed, "Please, God, if he's not the one for me, show me."

I called his sister the following day and told her he had been acting strange. She said, "Pam, I can't tell you what's going on, Mama is upset, and she told him that he needed to tell you." The Holy Spirit whispered the answer, and I said to her, "He got married, didn't he?" She said, "Well, he can't say I told you. Mama is furious with him for marrying that girl half his age. She put him out. She said he should have married you, not her." Surprisingly, I was hurt, but I wasn't destroyed by this news. I was relieved, and I released him. That soul tie had been broken. That was it for me. I felt at peace, he was behind me, and I was ready to move on. The Holy Ghost asked me, "Why would God want you to be with a man that doesn't serve him?" I knew that he was not a part of my destiny, and I could not allow him to stop me from getting there.

DAUGHTERS OF THE KING STOP KISSING FROGS

God revealed it to me, and it was clear, this man was part of the enemy's plan for my life. This was war and he wasn't going to win. He tried to come over and talk to me and I wouldn't entertain him. I got rid of everything he ever gave me, which wasn't much. I dropped it at his sister's house. I went through my house and prayed in every room. I began to get rid of furniture, clothes and shoes that had any ties to him or any other past relationship. I had entered into a phase of deliverance. I went by to see his mother and tell her goodbye. We sat and had a wonderful talk, and the Holy Spirit used me to minister healing to her and her relationship with her new daughter-in-law. I reminded her that the girl was only 23, and she had gone against her family to be with him. "He's going to disappoint her, and you will be the only family she will have to turn to," I told her. "Don't turn your back on her because of me. I am going to be fine," I said. "I will miss you, but I can't hold on to a relationship with you, he's married now. "She said, "He should have married you if he married anyone, it should have been you." I told her that God had other plans for my life, and I would be fine.

Three months prior to that day, my friend had moved back to Durham from Raleigh. It was in 2002 when she had moved back and relocated her bookstore. I went by to check out the store and have lunch with her one day. She invited me to come back around closing time. When I got off work, I went home, changed clothes and went to the store. I noticed my Godmother and one of her cousins were there, and they were having a discussion of the Bible. I picked up a Bible and sat down. About 30 minutes into the Bible study, a man walked in with two children. We continued the Bible study for another hour.

Afterward, I was walking around the store looking at books and music when the man came up to me. He asked me what my name was again, and I said, "Pam." I thought I must look like someone he knows. He walked away and came back. He looked at me and said, "God told me to tell you that he's going to heal you. I see that you have pain in your back, trouble sleeping and headaches. When you love, you love hard and he said, "tell her I'm going to mend her broken heart." He walked away, and a few tears had started flowing, but I wasn't ready to surrender. He came back to me and said, "God said that there are three people who owe you an apology, and because you walked away from one of them today and didn't say anything, He's going to bless you. I couldn't believe it! He was describing something that had just occurred that day at work. The person he was referring to had been talking about me to my ex-boyfriend and had the nerve to speak to me that day. The Devil said, "You ought to curse him out," but I didn't. An overwhelming sense of peace fell over me, and I surrendered my life to Christ that night. Since then, I have stumbled and fallen, but I never turned back. For three days, I was filled with love and forgiveness for all my enemies. I had an overwhelming desire to heal the hurting people. So I began to share Jesus with whoever would listen.

I still had things I needed to be delivered from. The desire to drink went away, but I still desired to smoke. I had some patches from a local program geared at helping people quit smoking. The funny thing is, I used the patch for over a year off and on until they stopped supplying them to me. Ideally, if a person wanted to quit, they would have quit by the first

three months. I was just using the patch to cut down on smoking. When I wanted to smoke, I took the patch off. This time I was determined to quit, and I called my friend to let her know how well I was doing on the patch. She said, "you don't need the patch. All you need is Jesus." Boy, did that make me mad. She didn't understand my plight. When she explained it to me, I understood. You see, if I really wanted to quit, all I had to do was pray and release that desire to God. I did that, and I have not smoked a cigarette since, nor have I used a patch.

The first book she gave me was "Destroying the Works of Witchcraft." When God broke that last boyfriend's soul tie, I began to really move forward with my life. He was married now, and I had moved on. He still tried to come by my house, and I wouldn't open the door. I told him to leave or I was going to call the police. He followed me and my friend to the grocery store one day. I spotted him sitting in his car in the parking lot, looking down on us. "I said to my friend, "he's here." She knew what I was dealing with, and she began to pray in tongues of war as we loaded the groceries. When she finished, and we looked up, he was gone. In August of that year, I was at home relaxing. I had just been dropped off by the church van, and I was fixing a bowl of ice cream when someone tried to kick my door in. My Pastor sent one of the ministers over from the church to secure the door after the Police left. They had snatched the outside screen door and broken the top hinge. Then they tried to kick open the inside door. When I screamed and ran to dial 911, I scared them away. I don't know if it was him or someone from the neighborhood who thought I was gone out, but I was ready to get out of that house. My cousin no longer lived across the street, and it just wasn't the same. I began fixing up the house to sell it, but I fell into financial troubles and ended up in foreclosure. One of my cousins recommended a friend in real estate who convinced me that she could sell my house to her investment group. I had signed a lease on an apartment and moved out when I found out they were not going to buy my house. This ended up being my way out. I simply walked away.

A few days before I moved out, I was getting ready to leave for work when there was a knock at my door. I asked," Who is it?" It was my ex again. I told him to go home to his new wife and leave me alone. He kept trying to talk to me through the door, and I just got quiet. When he saw that I wasn't responding to him, he must have been scared that I was calling the police, and he left. The day I moved out, I saw some guys working on renovating my cousin's old house. I went over there to check out the work, and I ended up asking them if they knew anyone who needed a brand-new refrigerator. That thing cost me about $1,000 after I finished paying it off. I loved it, but I couldn't take it with me. I didn't want to leave it in the house for the bank, so I ended up selling it for $96. I sold my small stereo for $40, and I had a little money in my pocket for food. When I moved into my apartment, I had no furniture except bedroom furniture and a dining room table and chairs. I had one chair in the living room that had a footrest. I would relax in that chair, watch TV and thank God for blessing me. I was at peace, even though I was still going through foreclosure. I was in a smaller apartment, and I had no furniture to sit on, and I was blessed. The weights had been lifted, and I was thankful to be in the place that I was in. God had started dealing with me in dreams. I started paying attention to and writing down all my dreams. Asia helped me through deliverance, and she continued with a ministry which had been birthed out of her store. The Pastor was a Prophet and very accurate. I learned a lot there, but I chose to go back to my home church. Before I left, the man I met at Bible Study that led me back to the Lord said that he saw me going back to school, getting on and off planes and some things that were not ready to be revealed yet. A few months later, I started attending The Garden of Prayer Bible College. It was part of The United Christian College and I learned so much while I was there. Thanks to all my instructors for their impartation into my life. At a service at another church, a Prophet from New York said that God's favor was all over me. I didn't know that meant I would suffer more than usual. I guess **Favor Ain't Fair**. One of the sisters in Christ ministered to me after the service. God had always dealt with me in dreams, I just didn't know it. I began writing down my dreams in 2002. Sometimes, I would forget to write them down, but I would remember later.

One dream that I had described three men, gave their initials, and told me the first two were not the ones. The last one God showed me, I thought He was showing me that he was the one. The other two came into my life and fulfilled the dream. The first one's initials were E.T. His first name began with an E and his last name began with a T. He came around Valentine's Day and asked me out. I was at work when he came into the Lobby and struck up conversation. He was tall, dark and muscular built. He was one big dude, just like I liked. He began to tell me about how he used to play Bass guitar in his aunt's church, but he hadn't been going to church. He was divorced and thinking about getting his life together. We talked for an hour while he tried to convince me to go out with him. When I found out his name, "ET, he's not the one, kept ringing in my head." I didn't go out with him.

A year later, a man from my past came into my life. My father had worked with him and he had tried to describe him over the years. He would run into him and he'd say, "That boy asked about you, he's always been crazy about you." I had no clue who he was talking about, but I thought about one guy I knew in high school. He came by to talk to my father one day and then he called me at work. At first, I was focused on the guy with the right initials and it wasn't him, so I declined his dinner invitation. I changed my mind a few days later, thinking that I was passing up a perfect opportunity to go out with a man that was interested in me. I did go out with him but when he confided that he was separated from his wife, I couldn't get past the Holy Spirit saying, "He's still married." I tried to make sense of my thoughts and ignore the Holy Spirit's gentle tugging in my spirit. After dinner, we talked a couple of times, but I suspected he wasn't telling me the whole truth, so I left it alone. Now, I didn't realize that he was the second man in my dream. His initials were M.M., and he was light-skinned. In my dream, he was represented by yellow M&M's raining from the sky. Wow, M.M. was his initials and also stood for married man. I dodged that bullet but barely. I was so lonely, I almost compromised for him. He was a minister and eventually, he would be single. I thought, "If she doesn't want him, I'll take him." There's always two sides to a story. The man that I thought was the one God was showing me didn't want me. The first time I saw him, there was a light around him that was awesome. My friend was talking to him and I asked her who he was. She said he was a friend of someone else we knew. It was the anointing that drew me to him. One of my co-workers tried to describe her cousin to me one day. She was asking me if I knew him. I didn't remember him; he was a few years older. A week later, I ran into him at a church service and I realized this was the guy she was talking about. He was also the guy that I had run into a few weeks earlier. Why did God keep showing me this man?

A house that I had been looking at with my brother and sister was a house that had been on the market for a while. I wanted to see that house and I always liked the house. I wasn't in the market for a house, but they were and I tried to get them interested but they weren't. I said, "God, I wouldn't mind living in that house myself." My co-worker told me that her cousin had bought a house. When she told me the name of the street, I described the house to her in detail. "He bought my house," I thought. When I ran into him at Walmart, I told him how I had been looking at that house for over a year and tried to get others to look at it. I said, " You bought my house!" He said, "You should have bought it, the owners kept records of all the upgrades and repairs. They really took good care of it." Out of curiosity, I asked him if the yard was fenced in. He looked at me kind of strange and he said, "No, but I was about to fence it in." I didn't mention to him that God had shown me the yard fenced in. We talked on and off for a couple of years, but it never really went anywhere. I had to face the fact that he wasn't interested. Whenever he showed interest in the past, there was always confusion. Missed calls at work, etc. His cousin always kept me informed but I knew there was a problem, and I knew what it was.

Around 2004, I started seeing this dark-skinned man in my dreams. He was always praying for the people and his eyes were red and piercing. They were like flames of fire. I had been praying for God to send a true Prophet to Durham that could reach the inmates, drug addicts, gang members, etc.

In April of 2009, I heard about a Prophet who had been in town running a revival. I went to the service with some church members after our Good Friday service ended. When I walked into the church, I noticed that the preacher was in jeans and a T-shirt. He looked kind of young and I thought, "Is this the Prophet?" Yes, it was- Prophet and Chief Apostle. He had just finished preaching and he started calling people out of the audience and prophesying to them. He was telling them about things that had happened in their childhood and diseases that were in their bodies, etc. When I went up, he told me about all the problems I was having in my health. He also told me that I had taken care of my family and God was going to bless me for that. Everything he said was amazing to me, and I couldn't help but notice that his eyes were red and piercing like the man in my dreams. His eyes fluttered like an eagle as he looked into the lives of the people. When he called people up for prayer, they were falling down when he embraced them. When I approached him, he asked if I was ready for a new anointing. As I braced myself, he embraced me. I felt a shock like a bolt of lightning go through my body. My shoes came off my feet and as I stood back up, he hit me again and said, "double portion." I was drunk in the spirit and he was laughing. A local Pastor opened her church for him to continue the revival and I tried to go every night. Eventually, I was working a full-time job, a full-time student and following the Prophet whenever I wasn't at my own church. When the Prophet started a ministry in Durham, I was there as much as I could be. Eventually, God led me to leave my family church and join his ministry. I had struggled with this decision for about a year. Words were coming from everywhere it seemed, confirming that it was time to go. One word that came from a Prophetess from Florida confirmed my decision. She said, "Prophetess, God sent me from Florida for you. Your enemies are under your feet, they lied on you and they had better be careful how they treated you." She went on about walking in my calling and not worrying about who didn't believe it. Wow, I thought, that's why God is trying to sit me under this Major Prophet. I will never get what I need from him if I don't sit under him. I have to go.

How can I leave my family church, my home church that I loved so much? One of the speakers that came to run revival told me that I should have been further along in my ministry by now, but I didn't walk through the door God opened for me. She said, "When God opens the door this time, you need to walk through it." I chose to walk through the door and trust what God was telling me and confirming through others. It was the hardest decision I had to make, but I had to find out what God had in store for me. I couldn't live my life for others, it was my time. Immediately, I thought I had made a mistake. The church was in constant turmoil and we began to go through major splits. In May of 2011, I graduated Valedictorian of my class in Bible College. The church continued to face its' hurdles, but I chose to remain faithful through it all. I loved the ministry and believed in the vision of my leader. Through much controversy, many trials and tests, I remained faithful and held on to what God had promised he was going to do for me. Everything was new and unfamiliar. It was an uncomfortable place to be. I didn't know these people and I wasn't used to making friends. It was hard to put myself out there. I had to come out of my comfort zone and risk rejection.

When my pastor was invited to preach in New Orleans, I was blessed to be able to travel with the man and woman of God. On the way to Louisiana, to a well-known Bishop's church, I remembered the man's words: "I see you traveling and getting on and off planes." I wondered what he saw that he didn't tell me and remembered him saying it wasn't time.

CHAPTER FIVE

Trials and Tribulations

Over the years, I had struggled with sickness in my body. There were phantom pains that would rip through my stomach, painfully heavy periods, backaches and extreme fatigue. I just always felt sick. I would see myself in a casket at an early age. In the dream, there were no children and no one to mourn my passing. At times, I was convinced that I would not make it to my forties. When I gave my life to Christ, I began to declare: "I shall not die, but live, and declare the works of the Lord"-*Psa 118:17*. Some years ago, I began to walk in healing and that's when the attacks on my body intensified.

In 2004, I had surgery to remove some fibroid tumors. One of my church members, "Lizz" was also in the hospital, on the same floor. She found out that she needed to go on Dialysis. When I returned home from the hospital, I became very sick. I called the Doctor and they gave me medication for nausea. A week later, I received a disturbing letter from the hospital. It sounded like something had gone wrong with the surgery at first, but the ending was worded like it was just a routine inquiry about the patients' welfare after surgery. Two weeks later, I went to church and "Lizz" asked me if I had heard what they had done to us in the hospital. I asked her what she was talking about. "You haven't seen it on the news," she asked? I hadn't watched the news regularly in years. I had no clue that Duke hospital had a mix-up with hydraulic fluid and surgical equipment. It was awful. Instead of laundry detergent used to clean and sterilize surgical equipment, hydraulic fluid was used. It had contaminated equipment in nearly 4,000 surgeries at two hospitals. Immediately, I thought about the sickness and nausea I had experienced. Also, as I researched it , I found out that my stiff joints were a common side effect reported by others who had been exposed. My joints had gotten so bad that I could barely get out of bed. My doctor sent me to a Duke Rheumatologist, who put me on medication for Rheumatoid arthritis. Lizz had found an attorney in Raleigh and I decided to consult them also. The lawsuit grew and right before they took it to court, they dismissed my case and Lizz's. They didn't feel they could win, they said. Eventually, Lizz grew sicker and kept getting staph infections. A couple of years later, she passed away. I stopped taking the medication when my doctor said he couldn't diagnose me with Rheumatoid arthritis. Whatever it was had seemingly gone into remission. The pain that was left was manageable with over-the-counter pain meds. I didn't like the idea of taking medications that were dangerous to my eyesight and I decided not to continue taking it, if I didn't have the condition. The tumors grew back, and I had another surgery in 2006. Over the next six years, I dealt with heavy bleeding and cramping associated with the tumors, which continued to grow. In 2010, the Doctors said I was anemic and in need of iron pills. The following year, I began to have shortness of breath and could hardly walk from the parking lot into the building for work. I got really sick and thought I had the flu or something. During that time, my cycle had started staying on for weeks. This time, it would not go off, so I started seeing a new Doctor. Over the weekend, I grew worse. I couldn't eat or stand up without getting dizzy. I was hemorrhaging and cramping really bad, my joints were aching, and my neck and back were hurting. I couldn't work or leave the house. At one point, I passed out from the pain and remember feeling like my spirit had left my body. God was trying to show me something. All I remember is maneuvering through twines and asking God why I was sick. He tried to show me three people, but I couldn't make out their faces. I prayed and bound the enemy and the works of witchcraft. The next day, I was able to get up and heat up some chicken noodle soup that one of my friends, sister Julia, had made for me. I forced myself to eat, it had been four days. My Doctor decided to give me a blood transfusion, since I was extremely anemic by this point, weak and steadily losing blood. I didn't want to take anyone else's blood and I cried to God about it. After receiving confirmation that he was going to give me a transfusion of the blood of Jesus, I went through with the procedure. After the transfusion, I was able to return to work. I felt much better, but I was still out of breath over a short walk. In the meantime, my Doctor tried pills, shots, etc., to stop the bleeding. Nothing worked and I soon had lost all the blood that had been transfused into my body. I had to have another surgical procedure and another transfusion. When I returned to work, I felt semi-brand new with the exception of my weight and blood pressure spikes. In 2012, I made the decision to have the gastric sleeve operation. My weight was hindering me, and I thought that it would help my neck and back if I could get some weight off. My neck and back were injured in a work-related incident in 2008 and the pain was excruciating. I wanted my life back and I set out to get it. Worker's Comp had released me back to work and declared there was nothing else they could do for me. I needed to lose weight. Well, I couldn't lose weight if I couldn't move or exercise. I was convinced I needed a neck brace to hold up my head at times. After dealing with worker's Comp for the last time, I accepted my fate and tried to deal with the pain as best as I could. When my neck would hurt, I would lay my head back. This would cause me to go to sleep. The Worker's Comp doctor said, "I don't know why that is, but I can see you've gained weight. You just need to stop eating." There it was again, the gnawing reminder that I was fat. My friend once said, "I had to get delivered from the word fat." I didn't quite understand what she meant but it truly is a struggle to get past that word and any insinuation that you eat more than the next person. I've seen skinny people who could eat much more than normal and not gain any weight. There was no stigmatism attached to their eating. If I picked up a piece of cake, I had to hear, "You don't need that." Eating bread was not good. I used too much sugar, etc., etc.

Although I was shapely, my weight climbed over the years. By this point in life, I couldn't exercise much at all, all my joints ached, and I was out of shape, struggling with severe neck and back pains. I could barely walk a short distance and I would not even go to the mall. The Doctor's evil comment cut like a knife and it enraged me, but I knew he was trying to make me feel like it was my fault. I knew that losing weight would help me feel better, but I felt hopeless in terms of being able to do it with diet and exercise, so I got medical help.

The people on my job have always picked on me and ostracized me. They tormented me for the entire time that I had worked there, so I decided to keep to myself and avoid their vicious attacks. They have always tried to pull me out of character and make me snap on them and I knew from a spiritual standpoint that it was going to intensify when I returned to work so I set out to avoid them. Over the years I have prayed for them and it reached a point where God wouldn't allow me to pray for some of them anymore. No man can bless what God has cursed. I had to kick the dust from my feet and move on. I believe God will bring them to their knees eventually and they will have to face themselves. It is not them anyway, it is the spirit that operates in them. I treat them the way I want to be treated. I love them, and I move on. When I am wrong, I repent and apologize. I can only answer for my actions. God will repay and he will make your enemies to be your footstools. There are several spirits in operation there, including the spirits of control, jealousy and manipulation. They are attached to witchcraft, sexual perversion and covetousness. Whenever I came up for promotion, someone high up in Security would black ball me and talk against my ability to handle the position. There were times when job descriptions were changed to fit someone else and keep me out. I have taken and passed tests and instead of being promoted, I have had the process opened back up before the year was up. I've had to work in a position for three months and have someone else get the promotion. The list goes on and on. There has been so much manipulation and cover up on my job. I worked in a hostile environment for over twenty-seven years.

I've been bullied in the workplace and kept from moving forward but God has the final word on that one and my enemies had better be careful for how they have treated the one person who prayed for their souls. For what shall it profit a man if he shall gain the world and lose his own soul; or what shall a man give in exchange for his soul?-*Mark 8:36.* The enemy uses people to come against the people of God and he uses people to come against you and keep you from God.

Exodus 6:1 Then the Lord said to Moses, Now you will see what I do to Pharoah: Because of my mighty hand he will drive them out of his country." When you become a born-again Christian, you are delivered from bondage and rescued from the spirit of Egypt. Egypt is a place of rebellion and wickedness against God. Taskmasters carry out the bidding of the spirit of Pharoah.

The Egyptian kings or Pharaoh means the son of the sun. They were considered as gods and the name Pharaoh was synonymous with the destruction of good things in infancy. This spirit can manifest as a strongman or principal-demon controlling a person, family, place or thing and bringing it under subjection to bondage. This spirit will never release a slave and will deprive them of freedom to reach their full potential for the Lord.

Like the Israelites enslaved in Egypt, I was bound to a job for over 27 years. 30 years and I would have reached full retirement, but God caused "the spirit of Pharoah" to drive me out. This is the story of my exodus.

I was branded in the infancy of my career, ostracized and hated without cause. I was also not saved. Eleven years later, when I gave my life to Christ, I stayed there to complete my assignment from the Lord. God positioned me in places throughout the rest of my career to minister to the "Israelites" still in bondage. Many began to seek the Lord as God instructed me to pray. Sometimes, God instructed me to fast and pray. I remember occasions where I had to fast three days with only water, specifically for co-workers who did not like me. One was having so much trouble. They were on the verge of breaking down. They continued to hate me and never knew I was praying for them. As the Lord positioned me, he also sent people to encourage me in that place. You see, I worked in the local county jail, and sometimes it was the inmates that had to encourage me in the Lord.

Although Down For The Count Volume II's chapter, "They Called Me Sarah." Dealt with infertility, I didn't go into detail about other struggles. In 2004 I was a victim of the Duke Hydraulic case and began to suffer joint pain and stiffness. I was placed on two medications that were dangerous to my eyes. A year later, the Rheumatologist said it wasn't RA.

In 2008, I was hurt in an incident involving a love triangle that clashed in a brawl in front of the Jail. Caught in the middle of two women trying to fight each other, I ended up taking the brunt of their blows. My shoulders and neck were injured, a slight tear to the meniscus of my right knee and lower back pain. For a week, I thought I could shake it off and continue working since I was stationed in the Control Room at the time (the place where officers on light duty were assigned when hurt anyway). But the neck pain was excruciating, so I had to report it. I got a cortisone shot for my knee and tried therapy for my neck.

After going back and forth with Workers Comp and getting nowhere, I was referred to Aqua therapy, which seemed to work for my neck. My therapist said she could tell I had been in a lot of pain because of the condition it was in. She worked on my range of motion and releasing the strain on my neck from where it was compacted, and I felt so much better, but I was released for the third time and decided to manage the pain as best as I could with heating pads and over the counter pain meds. About two years later, I went back to Workers Comp and ended up suing them. I didn't win because they said I didn't go to my Doctor for treatment and blamed my pain on degenerative arthritis. Even my doctor said I didn't have arthritis that wasn't normal for people my age, and the Rheumatologist couldn't diagnose Rheumatoid Arthritis. At this point in my career, I had about 20 years of service in, and I decided to return to work and deal with the pain. Eventually, after losing weight, my pain got better, but that was short-lived.

I had to deal with the taunts of others who felt like I wasn't hurt and that I always had an ache or pain somewhere. Well, I did! And being taunted about it started making me think maybe these pains weren't real. It seemed to get worse when I was stressed out, and I began to think back as far as I could to the beginning, tracing the source back to the back injury received during one-armed self-defense class in Jail School in 1992. I never reported it to my supervisor because I didn't know about Worker's Comp back then. I just started having severe back spasms and was prescribed muscle relaxers and pain medications. I thought it was due to me being top heavy, so I eventually had a breast reduction in 1998, which did help take the strain off my back.

In 2017, my Exodus began. You see, I had been in Egypt too long. I began having vertigo, and my Doctor suspected I might have had a stroke on the brain or an aneurism. As they began testing me to rule out these things, the medication I was on caused me to have trouble getting up in the mornings. I would come in late, and because I was temporarily assigned to another area that didn't require me to punch the clock, so to speak, I let my supervisor know and told him I was flexing the time I had built up from staying over in Courts which was pretty much every day. Pressure was placed on me from outside antagonists about this, and I was told there was no such thing as "flex" time, and I needed to come to work on time. I was still on medication and suffering headaches and vertigo when I was sent on a three-hour drive alone to pick up an inmate in another county. I prayed as I drove three hours there, picked up a female, and drove three hours back with no backup officer and no definitive answer to the cause of the vertigo. Everyone knew of the County directive to send two officers on trips outside the county, but no one cared. I was put in the position to refuse so that I could be written up. Many times, I was expected to produce "Bricks without Straw," so to speak, set up to fail. Pushed to the limits and dared to speak up.

The Facebook incident came next, where an employee of another agency of the County took my picture and placed it on Facebook with a derogatory caption. I was in Administration on a coffee break and sat down to drink a cup before Court started. I laid my head back and appeared to be sleeping when the pic was snapped. I was furious because the focus was on the appearance of me asleep and not on the pain it caused me, the embarrassment, and the lack of empathy I received. My co-workers taunted me, and what happened next, I honestly felt like it was intentional, and I felt bad for thinking that.

The door hit me on the left arm, and I walked on to my post. I called the Control Room to report it because my shoulder started aching, and I knew I would need another shot to calm the pain. I sent an email to my supervisors explaining the previous injury, and I worked the rest of the day and went to Urgent Care after work. The County flat out denied my claim saying the door didn't hit me. A month later, I was hit again, and I let them know it didn't hurt me, but they needed to be careful. I was cursed out in the background. I complained, and nothing was done. A month or so later, they hit me a third time.

God orchestrated these incidents to deliver me from this place. I wanted to stay for three more years, but God said no! He made it so I had to sue Worker's Comp, and in order to receive my settlement, I had to resign or retire. It was clear they wanted me gone, so I took early retirement, and I moved forward. I now know it was all part of God's plan for Pharaoh to let me go. I'm officially Out Of "Egypt," and I want to encourage you whatever place you are in -dealing with the spirit of Pharaoh, God himself will cause "Pharaoh" to release you. It was God's mighty hand that caused Pharaoh to drive me out!

In the early years, my enemies' taunting and plotting kept me bound by bitterness and hatred and kept me separated from God.

When I had my breakthrough, God gave me compassion to see my enemies freed too. It is their choice; they must be born again. I beseech you therefore, brethren, by the mercies of God, that ye present your bodies a living sacrifice, holy, acceptable unto God, which is your reasonable service- *Romans 12:1*. Though people continue to hate the God in me, I continue to pray for them. They are walking in darkness, blind to the very one who can save their souls. The choice is theirs; they must choose God for themselves. In the meantime, I had to realize that it is not them, but it is the spirit that is operating in them. I see their souls, and I cry out to God for their souls. You have to remember the state you were once in before God.

The parable of the rich man and the beggar Lazarus teaches us that you may gain the world and its riches, but if you die and lose your soul, what have you profited? Think about it: what can compare to eternal life? Fret not thyself because of evildoers- *Psalm 37:1.* They may seem to be prospering right now, but they will be brought down to nothing. For all of their haughtiness and blatant mocking of God, they will pay the ultimate price. That is why I pray for them because they don't know what they are doing. When you have been set free, you want everyone to be free. You are not free if you are still lying, still fornicating, still committing adultery, still homosexual, still backbiters, lovers of yourselves, etc. You can't practice sin and still reap the benefits of eternal life. If you have been born again, you are new creatures. The Holy Ghost keeps you from the power of sin, which means that you have the power to resist the temptations of sin. It's still your choice, but if you could do it on your own, you wouldn't need God.

CHAPTER SIX

Letting Go and Letting God

Life hasn't been easy for me. There were many times that I wanted to give up. I have held on to God's promises for the past eighteen years, it's all I had. I was crazy enough to believe God. God was going to mend my broken heart. He promised me. God was going to make my enemies my footstools. He promised me. God was going to take me before great men, he promised me. He was going to give me the desires of my heart. He promised me. When my house went into foreclosure, I was determined to let go and let God. My realtor convinced me that she would have my house sold to her investment group within a couple of weeks, so I decided to get an apartment and move out of my house. After I signed the lease, she informed me that the investors were not interested. My home went into foreclosure, and there was nothing I wanted to do about it. I could have saved it, but I didn't . God said, let it go, and I did.

I remember the day I moved out, there were some men working on my cousin's old house, and I asked if anyone needed a refrigerator. My refrigerator cost over $1,000, and I ended up selling it for $96. Most of my furniture had been given away, and I had started remodeling the house. The kitchen had new cabinets, new countertops and a new floor. As I looked around at what was left, it was sad, but at the same time, I felt peace about it. I knew God loved me, and it would work out for my good.

When I moved into my two-bedroom apartment, I had bedroom furniture and one black chair and footstool. Those were peaceful times, times when I was content to just be. I was starting over and letting go of the past. My healing had begun the year before when I had given my life to Christ and completely surrendered to his will. I released the pain of past relationships and embraced the Love of God. I began to walk in the Spirit and live for God. Although I was losing my first house and starting over from scratch with practically nothing, I was at peace. I was going to Bible College, working full time and working in my church. One by one, men from my past relationships began to reach out, and one by one I passed the test. I became obsessed with this crazy dream I had about three men that would come into my life. They were represented by initials. I was at work in the Lobby when a man came in. Tall, dark and very muscular built. It was around Valentine's Day, and I was feeling lonely. I had been waiting on God for a few years by this time, and nothing! My friends would laugh at me because I was so consumed with God that they said I missed it or didn't recognize when a man was trying to flirt with me. I was all kingdom business at the time and wasn't entertaining anything that walked like, looked like or resembled a "frog." It was like my eyes were shielded from even seeing them. This guy struck up a conversation, and at first, I was just enjoying the conversation and finding out we knew some of the same people. He then turned the conversation to something more personal and began to talk about himself and what he was looking for. It turns out he was divorced but still very close friends with his Ex. He played the Bass guitar and used to play for his church but was no longer going to church. Of course, he was thinking about going back, he said. I knew his Pastor and a few members of his home church, but when he asked me out, I could only hear a loud voice in my head saying, "NO!" He was really turning on the charm, trying to convince me that I didn't want to be alone for Valentine's Day, and I didn't, but I heard, "NO!" When he told me his name, I remembered the dream. His initials were ET, and in the dream, I associated these initials with the movie ET. That's how I remembered. In the dream, God was saying ET is not the one, not the one. I listened to the Holy Spirit and stuck to my answer, no thank you.

Not long after that, I got a call from a guy who always liked me, but I never dated. It turns out he knew my father, and he would always ask about me over the years. I remember my father talking about him and describing him, but he could never remember his name. He would always say that boy asked about you. Well, I thought it might have been him, but I hadn't seen him since my Junior year of High School. He had graduated that year and went into the Military. I wondered about him over the years but never saw him. He began to talk about how he had just spent half the day talking to my father and found out where I worked, so he decided to call me. At first, I said no to getting together but took his number. Eventually, I called him and agreed to go to dinner. He came by my apartment, and I was ready to eat. I was two weeks into the Atkins diet and hadn't eaten anything because we were going to go out. I was basically starving my body of sugar and carbs, and I felt like I could just open a packet of sugar and just eat it. When he arrived, he was checking out my garbage disposal and making small talk about himself. We sat down and talked a little bit, and he told me that he was separated from his wife. Separated? That means you're still married. He assured me she had moved on. I found out they were both Ministers, and from what he told me, the situation seemed awkward. I decided I didn't want any parts of drama, but against my better judgment and hunger pangs, I still went to dinner with him. As soon as we entered the restaurant, a man came up to him, greeted him, and said, "Playa, Playa- what's up, man?" That was the second sign, but the last sign was when his cousin came over and sat with us through the whole dinner, and he told her how much he always loved me and how he wasn't going to let me get away this time and all she said was, MMM...UHH HUH and nodded her head like "Really." I knew her, and she knew that I didn't have a clue, so I believe she wanted to protect my reputation, so to speak, by sitting with us. I decided not to see him again, but we stayed in contact. After a few weeks of talking on the phone, I decided I didn't trust him, and it was best to part ways until he made some decisions. His initials were MM, and in the dream, he was represented by bright yellow M&M's that were raining from the sky. Later after telling this story to a group of women, one of the older Pastors laughed and said M&M stood for married man.

The last man in the dream was a little fuzzy, but I met a man that I was convinced was him. From what I remember, this man was the one, but I couldn't remember his initials. When this one guy came along, I truly believe I made him fit the bill. Everything about him seemed to add up. But it wasn't so. I was asked by a mutual friend if I knew him, and I said no. The following week we crossed paths, and a few weeks after that, our paths crossed again. The acquaintance was trying to play matchmaker, or so it seemed, but we never hit it off. It's crazy how things turned out in that situation because our families had been intertwined for years, but I couldn't ever remember meeting him before that day. But timing always seemed to be off, and we could never get it together. I remember he called me at work one day, and I had just stepped out of the Control Room, and when I walked back in, one of the girls told me he had called and then kind of laughed. When I called him back, he wasn't receptive...never did find out what happened. My sister was looking for a house, and so was my brother, who had just moved back home. We were out looking at houses, and I took them by a house that I liked and had been looking at for about a year. I wasn't ready to get another house yet, but I tried to get one of them to make an appointment to look at it. They weren't interested. I would drive by there from time to time to see if it was still for sale. One day the mutual acquaintance was telling me that this guy had bought a house, and when she told me what street it was on, I began to describe it to her. Sure enough, it was my favorite house. God had shown me a fence around the house and a dog, so I asked him about it when I ran into him, and he told me that he was planning on fencing it in. When I try to remember the end of the dream about the three men, I can't remember what happened. All the signs pointed to him, but it wasn't.

As the years passed, I would get excited about the possibility of who he was. I was waiting in expectation for my husband. Prophecy after prophecy came about the husband and children I was going to have. Things I wanted more than anything else. You see, my biggest fear was to end up like my Aunt. She was the Pastor of the family church. She never married, she never had any children of her own, and she dedicated her life to serving others. She gave up her chances at having a personal family and life of her own to remain single and completely dedicated to God. If a man came along and didn't fit into her life or she would have to give up her church for, not a chance. I didn't want that life, and it seemed like that's what I ended up with after all.

In my first Anthology, Down For The Count Volume II, I wrote a chapter entitled, "They Called Me Sarah." This chapter recounts my struggle with infertility and fibroid tumors. Doctors wanted to give me a hysterectomy while prophecies came forth that I would have children. I refused the surgery while I struggled to walk in healing. Those years were very rough emotionally, mentally, spiritually and physically. I was drained on all levels. My body looked nothing like I was told could and would produce. I held out all hope until I felt like there was no real hope left. Yes, God can do anything, and I know that. I just had a Pastor on Facebook prophesy to me about some children, and he said I was supposed to have kids. What that means, I don't know. But everyone seems to want to call me Sarah like I'm going to have children in my old age. Well, I'm old now, and you can't get much older than this having kids. So I just had to let go of everything and let God have his way in my life. I stopped thinking about it and trying to figure it out and wondering if it's ET or MM or what's God got in store for me. I stopped asking why me?

CHAPTER SEVEN

I'll give up the Frogs Tomorrow

Galatians 6:7 Be not deceived; God is not mocked: for whatsoever a man soweth, that shall he also reap.

Exodus 8:1-10 1Then the LORD said to Moses, "Go to Pharaoh and say to him, 'Thus says the LORD, "Let My people go, that they may serve Me.2"But if you refuse to let them go, behold, I will smite your whole territory with frogs.3"The Nile will swarm with frogs, which will come up and go into your house and into your bedroom and on your bed, and into the houses of your servants and on your people, and into your ovens and into your kneading bowls.4"So the frogs will come up on you and your people and all your servants.""5 Then the LORD said to Moses, "Say to Aaron, 'Stretch out your hand with your staff over the rivers, over the streams and over the pools, and make frogs come up on the land of Egypt.'"6So Aaron stretched out his hand over the waters of Egypt, and the frogs came up and covered the land of Egypt.7The magicians did the same with their secret arts, making frogs come up on the land of Egypt.

God sent down 10 plagues (signs and wonders) from Heaven to show His power and bring judgment on Egypt. The second plague was that of frogs. Frogs are also used as symbols of disgust due to their moist skin that can be perceived as slimy and the sometimes-repugnant secretions, especially of toads. In the Bible (Exodus 8:6), the Second Plague of frogs is sent upon Egypt; as a deliberate irony by the God of Moses, as the Egyptians saw frogs as a symbol of life and worshiped a frog-goddess. Later, frogs are also associated with unclean spirits in Revelations 16:13.[2]

The Biblical plague of frogs sent to curse ancient Egypt, like the nature of the other plagues, was intended to show the sovereignty of the God of Moses over the gods of Egypt.

8 Then Pharaoh called for Moses and Aaron and said, "Entreat the LORD that He remove the frogs from me and from my people; and I will let the people go, that they may sacrifice to the LORD."9Moses said to Pharaoh, "The honor is yours to tell me: when shall I entreat for you and your servants and your people, that the frogs be destroyed from you and your houses, that they may be left only in the Nile?"

10 Then he said, "Tomorrow." So he said, "May it be according to your word, that you may know that there is no one like the LORD our God.

The frog is special to the Egyptians because they worship a female deity Heqet with a frog's head. This god is connected with nature worship in Egypt and had something to do with the annual flooding of the Nile. Later, as a fertility goddess, associated explicitly with the last stages of the flooding of the Nile, and so with the germination of corn, she became associated with the final stages of childbirth. This association, which appears to have arisen during the Middle Kingdom, gained her the title She who hastens the birth. Although there was no ancient Egyptian term for "midwife" known for certain, they often called themselves the Servants of Heqet, and her priestesses were also trained in midwifery. Women often wore amulets of her during childbirth, which depicted Heqet as a frog, sitting in a lotus.

When these frogs came up, all the Egyptians would understand that there was a God greater than their god who was able to control their god. God uses the things of this world to confuse and confound the people of this world. But Pharoah, seeing that God was more powerful than Heqet, chose to spend one more night with the frogs. We are given the opportunity to give our lives to Jesus, accept him as savior, and receive all of God's promises. Our response is tomorrow, God. God is saying Tomorrow is not promised!

In medieval Europe, the frog was a symbol of the devil due to the Catholic church associating the frog as one of the animal's witches use as a familiar. Exodus deals with many plagues. The second plague is the plague of the frogs. Frogs were seen as a symbol of fruitfulness and fertility. The frog in areas near the Nile had been deified. Because of the high standing of frogs in the community, killing a frog intentionally carried a sentence of death. Killing frogs accidentally could also result in death. So, when the plague of the frogs came, not only was it drastically inconvenient to the people of the town, not a single one of the beasts could be killed. This was meant to teach the people believing in false deities would not be tolerated and served as yet another battle between the Pharaoh and God.

Frogs represent uncleanness. The river of Egypt (the Nile) caused many plagues and illnesses throughout the years. Unsanitary practices with food caused many deaths from food leading to a good portion of the kosher food doctrine. Frogs arose from the unclean river, making the animal dirty as it came from the tainted river.

Croaking represents the denial of Divinity. The croaking of frogs represents the naysayers of divinity. The sound of the noise keeps the truth from reaching those who need to hear the information. Psalms discuss Egypt's river bringing forth frogs upon the land. This is seen as an evil that comes to ruin the world. In addition, the croaking represents grabbing all the good out of life and not worrying about your eternal soul, a Do as you please attitude, a live for the moment attitude.

Frogs were called Marsh Leapers. The marsh leapers were not to be trusted. The idea an animal could live in two worlds, both the water and on land, was not understood at the time. Frogs became the symbol of someone who could not commit to a belief system. This alluded to being tempted by the devil or the unclean ways of the less than devout.

I saw out of the mouth of the dragon, and out of the mouth of the beast, and out of the mouth of the false prophet, three unclean spirits, like frogs; for they are the spirits of demons, working signs to go forth unto the kings of the earth, and of the whole world, to gather them together unto the war of the great day of God Almighty (**Rev. 16:13, 14**)

The nation of Israel was enslaved in Egypt. God had sent Moses to tell Pharaoh to set Israel free and let them leave Egypt. Pharaoh had refused, so God began to send plagues upon the land of Egypt as a means of changing Pharaoh's mind. The second plague was frogs. They were innumerable. Think about the problems the plague of frogs brought to Egypt. The frogs were everywhere! Frogs in the bedroom, frogs in the kitchen, frogs in the parlor, frogs in the oven, frogs in the yard! God had said,

> **"If you refuse to let the children of Israel go, behold I will smite all your borders with frogs." Exodus 8:2**

God keeps His word. Think about it, an Egyptian woman opening her oven; she screams and out jumps frogs! When they pulled down the sheets to get into their beds, frogs are all over! Trying to put on clothes and frogs are in your pockets? Frogs! Frogs in the palace! Frogs in the huts! Little frogs! Big frogs! The sound of croaking must have been so loud and unbearable. Frogs in the house, frogs in the yard, thousands of dead frogs heaped up in smelly mountains as millions more came from the rivers to take their place! Finally, Pharaoh could stand it no longer. He called for Moses, the Servant of God.

> **"Entreat the Lord, that He may take away the frogs from me, and from my people; and I will let the people go, that they may do sacrifice unto the Lord."**

Now Moses was overjoyed. At last, Pharaoh had made up his mind to obey the Lord. Finally, Moses thought that Pharaoh could see clearly. Surely Pharaoh could see that God was God. So Moses said,

"Glory over me, when shall I entreat for thee, and for thy servants, and for thy people, to destroy the frogs from thee and thy houses, that they remain in the river only?"

And here is Pharaoh's unbelievable answer. Pharaoh said, "Tomorrow!"

Can you believe it? I can't figure that one out! If you had Frogs in your food, frogs in your bed, frogs in your clothes, frogs everywhere and God was ready to remove the frogs instantly, and the decision was up to you, Would you have said, Tomorrow? It was as though he was saying, "Give me one more night with the frogs." How could he possibly have chosen one more night with those frogs? It was a strange decision on Pharaoh's part.

What about the frog situation in your own life? We have them, you know. I'm talking about the frogs of troubles, doubt, burdens, suffering, sickness, sorrow, perplexities, disappointments and heartaches. Frogs! All of them! Frogs of difficulty and grief on every hand. They plague us morning, noon and night. They are a constant source of harassment. Why do we choose to stay in misery with the frogs? Why do we inflict punishment on ourselves?

Moses was sent by God to deal with the frog problem in Egypt. Jesus was sent by God the Father to deal with the frog situation in our lives. God was standing by. He was ready to remove the frogs that troubled the Egyptians; whenever they were willing to ask. Likewise, the Lord is standing by, ready and willing to help us deal with the troublesome frogs of our life whenever we are willing to ask Him to intervene. Tomorrow God, I've got to get myself together first. Tomorrow Lord, I must tie up some loose ends. Tomorrow God, I'm waiting on someone else. Tomorrow Lord, tomorrow..... God said tomorrow is not promised. Stop putting up with frogs. It's time to let go and let God.

Letting Go and Letting God has been hard. I suffered many disappointments over the past 18 years, and I'm still suffering disappointments. It's hard to describe the feeling of being lonely when you're a loner by nature. I wanted a husband and a family, and each year that passed by left me feeling like it would never happen unless I made it happen. Just like Tamar in the Bible, who married all the brothers but never got the last husband or baby that was promised, so she took things into her own hands.

One more night with the frogs. That last soul tie-Lil Man. The one I allowed to stomp on me. I hadn't seen him in years. I had kept my distance for a reason. I would always fall for his croaking. I would always want to believe that he was changed. I would always love him, and he knew it. Years had passed, and there he was in front of me in the grocery store in the area where I had moved to. It turned out he lived a few miles away, and we had been in the same area for a few years. We started talking, and something seemed so different about him and promising that I felt safe. I overlooked all the signs and decided I was going to make things happen for myself. I was ready to go for it, and I didn't care what anyone thought. I was on assignment, and I took a detour off course. When things didn't work out, I asked him to forgive me because my job was to minister to him. He never understood that, of course. After going back and forth for a while, he moved on to someone else. He hadn't changed after all.

Most of them I find are still the same Marsh jumping, not to be trusted, double life, unbelieving, loud croaking frogs they have always been- just disguised it better. Every time I think about him now, all I hear is Ribbit, Ribbit, Ribbit! After dealing with frogs and going through deliverance from the frogs in my life, I chose to spend one more night with the frogs!

After this final heartache I had inflicted on myself, I had to take a look at myself. I had to examine myself. Why had I continued to make these choices? Who was I choosing over and over again in these men? What was I looking for? Why was I not finding it? I discovered that it wasn't them. It was me. I was choosing men that I thought I could rescue and turn into a Prince. Just like in the fairy tale- she was the Princess, and he was just a frog until her kiss turned him into the Prince. I was choosing frog parts and trying to piece together a man. Only God can take a broken man and bind his wounds. And as it was ministered to me so profoundly by one of my keynote conference speakers, God never promised us a prince anyway- the man is supposed to be the Priest of his home. I also had to look at the broken little Princess and realize that her crown was cracked too. She needed God to repair and restore what was broken before she could be ready for him.

This book is not written to bash the men who played a role in my life. They were not frogs. It was the identification of characteristics of the unclean spirits operating in them that were explored in this book. You see, if truth be told, I was never their idea of a Princess either. This is written to all the Daughters of the King who finally know who they are in Christ and are waiting on God's promise... It may not come when you want, but it will be right on time.... Stop Kissing Frogs!

About the Author

Elder Pamela Horne was born the fourth child of eight in Island County, Washington State. She was raised and educated in Durham, NC. A woman of God with a compassion for ministering to broken women, she has a heart for seeing men and women delivered, restored and renewed in Christ.

In 1988, she earned a Bachelor's degree from Western Carolina University in Radio/TV and Journalism. She received a Bachelor's degree in Christian Education and Biblical Studies in 2011 from the Durham Extension of the United Christian College of Goldsboro, NC.

Elder Horne began her ministry under Pastor Dr. Mae V. Horne of Gateway To Heaven UHCA. She was ordained under Chief Apostle William D. Lee in 2012. In 2015, her vision for Consuming Fire Ministries was birthed. She loves the Lord and continues her ministry work at Gateway To Heaven, UHC, under the leadership of Pastor Marian Freeman-Weaver.

In 2019, she was ordained as an Elder in the UHCA. She recently retired after over 27 years of service to the Sheriff's Department. Currently, she serves as the Co-Director and Event Planner of The

Women of Triumph Ministries. She is a true worshipper and loves music & singing.

As a single woman with no children, one of her favorite scriptures is **Romans 12:1** *I beseech you therefore, brethren, by the mercies of God, that ye present your bodies a living sacrifice, holy, acceptable unto God, which is your reasonable service.* She strives to live this scripture out in her life that others may see the Christ that lives inside of her.

His Glory Creations Publishing, LLC is an International Christian Book Publishing Company, which helps launch the creative works of new, aspiring and seasoned authors across the globe, through stories that are inspirational, empowering, life-changing or educational in nature, including poetry, journals, children's books, fiction and non-fiction works.

DESIRE TO KNOW MORE ABOUT HGCP?

Contact Information:
CEO/Founder: Felicia C. Lucas
www.hisglorycreationspublishing.com
Facebook: His Glory Creations Publishing
Email: hgcpublishingllc@gmail.com
Phone: 919-679-1706